PRAISE FOR *ACT LIKE YOU MEAN BUSINESS*:

"I adore this book; it's chock full of very useful advice about how to communicate successfully for businesspeople AND anyone! It should be required reading for every Fortune 500 CEO."
TIM SCHELLHARDT, SENIOR VICE PRESIDENT, EDELMAN PUBLIC RELATIONS AND FORMER BUREAU CHIEF, *WALL STREET JOURNAL*

"Rob's characteristic savvy and wit come through loud and clear in this insightful and practical handbook for leaders. It's a great read and even greater resource!"
MARIL MACDONALD, FOUNDER AND PRESIDENT, GAGEN MACDONALD

"A really fascinating read. I've seen many teachers and authors attempt to legitimize the arts in a business context, but Rob really succeeds in a casual, entertaining fashion."
ROB KOZLOWSKI, ONLINE REPORTER, CRAIN COMMUNICATIONS, ADJUNCT FACULTY MEMBER, COLUMBIA COLLEGE CHICAGO; AND FORMER ASSOCIATE FACULTY MEMBER, SECOND CITY TRAINING CENTER

"Both business and acting have their share of drama, but *Act Like You Mean Business* captures their intersection perfectly. Whether writing the 'About Us' section for a website or checking your fear during a crisis, this useful guide offers lots of practical advice and is like having your very own pocket communicator."
PETE BRACE, MARKETING/COMMUNICATIONS CONSULTANT AND FORMER COMMUNICATIONS DIRECTOR, GATORADE

"Rob's experience as an actor and communications professional help drive home the point that communicating, in whatever format, is a kind of performance whose success is not measured in applause, but reaction, responsiveness or simple understanding. It's a great read."
JOHN KEIGHTLEY, VICE PRESIDENT, DEVELOPMENT, CAMPAIGN FOR TOBACCO FREE KIDS

"Pulling from real-life case studies, notable literature and authors, and his love of TV, film, and live theater, Rob unpacks those insanely hard to master 'Soft Skills' in an entertaining, educational, and wonderfully thought-provoking book!"
BOB KULHAN, CEO, BUSINESS IMPROVISATIONS LLC

"Good communication is everyone's responsibility. And this book shows how to apply scores of techniques from the world of film, TV, and theater, so we can all communicate much better. A profound, yet entertaining, read."
MICHAEL FREEBORN, FOUNDING PARTNER, FREEBORN & PETERS

ACT LIKE YOU MEAN BUSINESS

ESSENTIAL COMMUNICATION LESSONS FROM STAGE AND SCREEN

ROB BIESENBACH

BRIGANTINE MEDIA

Act Like You Mean Business

Published by Brigantine Media
211 North Ave., St. Johnsbury, Vermont 05819

Cover and Book Design by Jacob L. Grant

ISBN 978-0-9826644-4-5

Other Brigantine Media books include:
It's About Time by Harold C. Lloyd
The Big Picture: Essential Business Lessons from the Movies
by Kevin Coupe and Michael Sansolo
Am I The Leader I Need To Be? by Harold C. Lloyd
Business Success in Tough Times by Neil Raphel, Janis Raye, and Adrienne Raphel
Win the Customer, NOT the Argument by Don Gallegos
Selling Rules! by Murray Raphel
Crowning the Customer by Feargal Quinn

For more information on these books please contact:
Brigantine Media
211 North Avenue, St. Johnsbury, Vermont 05819
Phone: 802-751-8802
Email: neil@brigantinemedia.com
Website: www.brigantinemedia.com

To my mother and father and Ed and Deb,
who taught me to work hard,
think critically,
laugh often,
and not be such a jerk all the time.

ACT I: EXPRESS YOURSELF

From the cave painters to Tony Soprano, everybody's got a story. Summon it, shape it, tell it.

In acting, emotion is everything. In business, it's a dirty word. But facts will only get you so far. Six tips for pumping up the emotion.

More than words. What we can learn from David Mamet, Jon Hamm, and Austin Powers.

ACT II: PLAY TO YOUR AUDIENCE

Vincent Vega's trying really hard to listen—so should we. Eight ways to be a better listener.

Before stepping onto the stage—literally or figuratively—think about your audience's expectations, mood, and interests, and how to connect with them.

Audiences crave authenticity. And just like a character's dialogue, every person and organization has a voice. Tips for capturing tone, rhythm, and style.

ACT III: A Script That Really Performs

INTERMISSION

ACT IV: Get Me Rewrites!

ACT V: ACTION!

ACT VI: THE BIG PICTURE

ENCORE

CURTAIN CALL

CURTAIN UP

Two roads diverged in a wood. And I took them both.

After many years in business, I decided to try my hand at acting. What began as a side interest soon developed into a second full-time career.

But a funny thing happened on the way to becoming an actor. The more I studied and performed, the more I realized that business and acting are not so different.

Connecting with an audience, expressing ideas visually, appealing to emotion, telling stories—these are all important lessons business people can use to communicate more persuasively and effectively.

As clients began to expect more creative approaches to communications, these two paths started to converge. Or maybe they were just one path the whole time.

Either way, it's been a good road. And that has made all the difference.

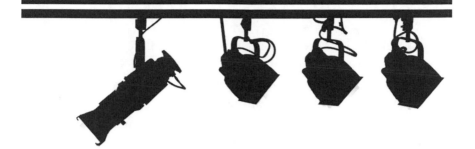

PREVIEW

he CEO was generally an amiable guy, but I'd never seen him as angry as he was that morning when he looked me in the eye and demanded, "What do we do now?"

Good question.

Moments before I was among the staff watching helplessly at the back of the room as employee after employee interrupted his presentation and peppered him with hostile questions. It all came to a head when a very large, very angry man rose from his chair, red in the face, to loudly berate the CEO, calling him incompetent and a liar, among other things, before storming out of the room.

I thought, hey, don't look at me, I just...well, I wrote the speech. And I was part of the team that enthusiastically sent the CEO there that day. But this was not how things were supposed to go.

The Best-laid Plans of Flacks and Men

It was the kickoff event for a series of town hall meetings that were the cornerstone of our communications strategy. The company was in dire straits—getting beat by the competition and beaten down by Wall Street—and the CEO was determined to turn things around.

But first he had to win the support of employees who had, over the years, grown increasingly distrustful and hostile toward management. We knew it would be a tough sell, but we weren't prepared for this.

When it was over, I was a little shell-shocked. I didn't know employees could get away with yelling at their CEO! (Such a naïve kid. These were union guys—they weren't afraid of anything. Except maybe NAFTA.)

The good news was we had a whole twenty minutes to figure things out before the next meeting was scheduled to start!

So we all thought hard about what to do. I retraced our steps. The presentation was well vetted. It laid out in stark terms the challenges and threats the company faced, and outlined a clear, factual, logical path to recovery. But something was missing.

The Metaphorical Nose on My Face

It was then I realized that the thing that was missing was right in front of us the whole time. Literally. Right there in the room was a full-scale model of the big diesel engine the workers produced in that plant. That was the key.

So I suggested to the CEO that before starting the next presentation, he should take a moment and talk about that engine. "Tell those workers what it means to you," I said. "You began your career right here in this plant. You helped design that engine. You've been with this company for almost thirty years. Why are you here today? Why are you fighting so hard for this company's survival?"

And that was it. The second presentation was pretty much identical in content to the first one, but those opening moments changed everything. The tone and the mood of the room shifted 180 degrees.

Okay, maybe 120 degrees. They didn't give him a standing ovation or clap him on the back and invite him out for beers. But no one walked out, either. No one shouted. They asked tough questions, yes, but they did it respectfully. And a few of those tough old union guys actually went up and thanked him for coming to see them.

Acting!

I didn't realize it at the time, but in that second presentation the CEO was putting on a performance. He was *acting*. And not in a cynical, fake way. He was embodying the most positive lessons we can take from the world of acting. Among them:

> ■ He connected with his audience on their terms. Those guys may have hated management, they may have hated him, but they loved those engines. And they loved the fact that he loved them, too.
>
> ■ He humanized himself, by revealing a personal side that they never expected to see.
>
> ■ He told a story, talking about his early career working in that plant and the challenges he faced.
>
> ■ He used emotion and tapped into theirs, by talking honestly and authentically about the pride they shared in the company's products and heritage.
>
> ■ He raised the stakes, pledging to fight for the company and for their future. A company that was founded at the dawn of the Industrial Revolution sure as hell wasn't going down on his watch!
>
> ■ And he expressed himself visually, using the engine—a prop, essentially—to impress an indelible image in their minds of what they were all there for, and what connected them to each other.

I didn't put all these pieces together at the time, of course. I just thought it was a really cool moment. (And I was super-relieved that I would have a job the next morning.)

But years later as I pursued my acting career, it dawned on me that this was a whole new way of viewing communications in the corporate setting.

LOOKING FOR INSPIRATION IN ALL THE WRONG PLACES

Too often in business we look for ideas from the usual cast of characters—colleagues, competitors, and others in our industry.

We scan their websites, go through stacks of annual reports, review award submissions, play videos, collect print pieces. Then we swipe the ideas we like best.

And while it can be helpful to measure yourself against your peers, always looking for inspiration in the same old places and from people just like us is a surefire recipe for blandness and sameness.

THERE'S NO BUSINESS WITHOUT SHOW BUSINESS

Instead of looking at other businesses, we should be looking at show business. After all, the most vibrant, compelling, and popular forms of mass communication include:

- Film, which draws a big enough audience to earn $10 billion in annual domestic revenue
- Television, which the average American spends 150 hours a month watching
- Live theater, which attracts a much smaller but highly passionate audience to thousands of venues, from Broadway to regional playhouses to gritty urban storefronts

This notion of looking to the entertainment world for creative inspiration is not without precedent. Shortly after the September 11 terrorist attacks, the government brought in Hollywood producers and screenwriters to help intelligence experts imagine, and thus better prepare for, the kinds of plots that might emerge next.

And back in World War II, the British government hired a bestselling novelist to devise and spin elaborate yarns—full-blown cover stories—to deceive the Germans about Allied operations, including the timing and location of the D-Day invasion.

Surely if an otherwise hide-bound institution like government can dare to look outside itself for creative approaches to problems, we can, too.

EVERYBODY COMMUNICATES

When I say "we," I mean everybody. It doesn't matter whether you're a doctor, a bookkeeper, or a store clerk. A line worker on the plant floor or an executive in the C-suite. Communication is everyone's responsibility, whether or not it's in the formal job description.

I worked with a CEO once who said that at least 50 percent of his job involved communicating—motivating employees, talking to the media, presenting to the board, speaking to investors, chatting up distributors, helping guide the branding strategy...it's all communications.

When it comes to linking acting principles to business, most people think about public speaking. But these lessons go way beyond speeches and presentations. They can also be applied to marketing materials, memos, videos, e-mails, tweets, and websites. Not to mention meetings, phone calls, job interviews, performance reviews, and hundreds of other things.

In fact, just about everything in business involves communication, from the way we answer the phone to how we carry ourselves to the color scheme we choose for our workplace.

You may not know it, but you're communicating right now. Is your door open or closed? Are you wearing a suit or jeans? Are you reading this in hard copy or as an e-book? All of that communicates something about you.

Using This Book

Act Like You Mean Business takes the best lessons from the world of film, television, and theater and applies them to business. It combines observations and insights from my study of acting, improv, and writing for the stage and screen with examples from my years in the corporate world. And it provides practical applications of the lessons in each chapter.

Finally, it does all this in a way that I hope puts into practice the things I preach: presenting useful information without putting you to sleep. Neither a dense textbook nor a sappy self-help tome, it's the kind of book that I would want to read.

Now, on with the show!

ACT

I I I I

EXPRESS YOURSELF

"A lot of this is theater. How do you communicate to 38 million people? You're not sitting down talking to them. So it's gesture, symbol, the narrative, the drama. Who's the protagonist? Who's the antagonist?"

—Jerry Brown, Governor of California

SCENE 1
THE POWER OF STORY

torytelling isn't just for novelists and screenwriters and playwrights. If you do any kind of communicating in your day-to-day work then you are in the storytelling business. At least you should be, if you want your audience—whether customers or colleagues—to take notice, pay attention, and absorb what you have to tell them.

Throughout time and across cultures, people have been communicating through stories—imparting beliefs, reinforcing values, giving meaning and structure to seemingly random, unconnected bits of information.

People crave stories. In fact, as my colleague Jim Signorelli points out in his upcoming book, there is scientific evidence that our brains are hardwired for stories. He cites the work of Kendall Haven, who says, "The steady diet of stories that children experience modifies the brain to render it more predisposed to think in story terms" (*Story Proof: The Science Behind the Startling Power of Story*).

The power of storytelling is something that celebrated filmmakers and fiery orators and everyday grifters figured out a long time ago.

What Is a Story?

There are lots of different definitions of story. In his research, Jim actually counted eighty-two separate definitions. He ultimately landed on one that's pretty similar to what we were taught in the writing classes I took at Chicago's Second City Training Center.

In the simplest terms, a story involves a character struggling to achieve a goal in the face of difficult odds or obstacles.

I was working with a client on a project designed to highlight the company's open, supportive culture. We interviewed employees about life in the firm and found some great stories.

One said, "My son pitches in Little League. Getting to his games means a lot to me, especially as a single parent. Here I feel comfortable taking off a little early to do that. Other places aren't that flexible." Our character here is a single father whose goal is to spend more time with his family. The obstacle is that most workplaces make carving out such time difficult.

Another employee described a huge, last-minute project in which one of the top partners helped her meet her deadline by staying late to help seal and stamp envelopes. The character is an overworked admin. Her goal is to meet her deadline and the obstacle is the strict hierarchical structure at most companies that impedes this kind of collaboration across levels.

Stories like these rise above the typical platitudes issued by corporate: "We promote work/life balance" or "We value teamwork." Stories bring to life the everyday struggles and triumphs we all recognize, delivering greater impact.

CHARACTER COUNTS

At the heart of every good story is a character we can relate to. And the best characters are multi-dimensional. They're recognizably human.

Take Tony Soprano. He's a man in a violent business, but he also shows deep love for his family, has a charming affection for animals, and suffers from debilitating panic attacks. We love Tony Soprano because he's complex and richly drawn and we can identify with him (not the violence and killing so much, but the daily anxieties and struggles with relationships and work).

Contrast that with, say, any villain in your typical James Cameron epic. The snooty rich guy in *Titanic*, for instance, or the ruthless military commander in *Avatar*.

What do we see? A caricature, not a character. Relentlessly evil with few, if any, redeeming or mitigating qualities. These people apparently are nasty just for the sake of it, which is not terribly interesting because it's not very believable.

OH, THE HUMANITY!

People who lead an organization or a team or face an audience need to be humanized. We can do that by showing a surprising side of their character that others don't often see. Or by highlighting qualities people can relate to—love of family, pets, hobbies, or sports, for instance.

I interviewed a factory worker in a plant that makes candy and gum. I asked her how she ensures a quality product. She walked me through all the steps, from inspecting for impurities to proper packaging to machine maintenance.

Then I asked about her children. "They must think you have a pretty cool job," I said. She lit up.

"Oh yeah," she replied, turning over a package of gum and pointing to a series of numbers and letters on the label. "See this code? It tells you exactly where this gum was made, right down to the production line. My kids will go into the candy aisle of a store, check out the label and say, 'This is Mommy's gum!'"

This woman is working hard to produce a quality product, because her customers are not only like family, they *are* family. It's good enough for yours because she makes sure it's good enough for hers.

Now *that's* a story.

STORIES ARE EVERYWHERE: WE JUST NEED TO FIND THEM

When you're presenting yourself to an audience—whether it's on paper, on camera or live—you need to go mining for your inner stories. Here are some questions to help you uncover them and discover what you're really passionate about.

- ■ Work-related:
  - □ What do you love about your job?
  - □ What's your favorite moment of the day?
  - □ What makes you proud?
  - □ What makes you jump out of bed in the morning to come to work?
  - □ Where does your job fit in the big picture?
  - □ How does it help achieve the organization's goals?
  - □ Describe a challenge you've faced.
    - • How did you overcome it?
    - • What were the keys to success?
    - • How did resolving it make you feel?
- ■ Personal:
  - □ What are your hobbies or interests?
  - □ What does your family mean to you?
  - □ What do your kids think you do?
  - □ What did you want to be when you were growing up?
  - □ What did you study in school?
  - □ Who are your heroes and why?

This approach also works when you're putting the spotlight on someone else—a customer or employee, for instance. Posing these types of questions helps open people up and draws out their stories.

THEN WE HAVE TO SHAPE THEM

In the book *Story*, which is widely considered the bible of screenwriting, author Robert McKee talks about causality versus coincidence. Causality involves events that are related and interconnected, thus providing meaning. Coincidence describes random events that have little impact on or relation to each other.

Causality makes for a better, more satisfying story. If your "character" is a firebrand CEO who shakes things up wherever he goes, then a story about him getting kicked out of prep school for defying authorities is an illuminating tale. His decision to study Spanish in college because he felt it was the easiest language to learn is less compelling—it doesn't reinforce the point you're making about what a rebel he is.

AND NARROW THEM

Another big part of shaping a story involves separating the meaningful wheat from the merely distracting chaff. We've all been subjected from time to time to the agony of a story chock full of unnecessary tangents and useless detail.

Like the meaningless date. Not to mention the even more meaningless one-sided debate about the date: *was it March or April? I think it was April. No, wait, it was snowing, so it must have been March...*

And the elevation of bit players to leading roles, complete with formal introductions and needless biographical data.

We're not making a documentary here. In fact, even documentary makers don't document every detail. They tell stories. And they know that facts—especially the unnecessary ones—can be the enemy of a good story.

Finally, We Have to Tell Them

How best to tell the story?

Just as there are a million stories in the big city, there are a million ways to tell them. Some are covered in this book—understanding audiences, tapping into emotion, using precise and evocative language. (And, as we'll discuss later on, one of the best ways to tell a story is to show it.)

Some of my favorite modern storytellers are Malcolm Gladwell, author of *The Tipping Point* and *Blink*, and the geniuses behind *Freakonomics*, Stephen Dubner and Steven Levitt. These bestselling authors manage to craft riveting tales out of obscure topics like the factors that motivate sumo wrestlers to cheat or how Hush Puppies suddenly became a major nationwide fad.

They've mastered an approach journalists use to draw readers in. They start small, on a very personal, human scale, focusing on a lone individual or a simple detail. Then they blow it out into a full-fledged story that illuminates a larger truth or trend.

They understand that anecdotes and examples help bring facts and statistics to life.

That's Entertainment

A major insurance company sought to encourage teens to drive safely. Instead of doing a standard PSA campaign, they created a seven-part web series—a whole mini-drama with characters and stories and action.

Messages about the hazards of texting and driving or drinking and driving were incidental to the story. The company knew that to reach their audience, they had to entertain them.

Whatever you write, whether it's a case study or the "About Us" section of a website or a blog post, seek first to entertain. Informing and persuading are important, of course, but if you put the reader to sleep, you'll never get that chance.

THE POWER OF STORY

Because they reveal something about ourselves that others can relate to, stories have unrivaled power for breaking down barriers between people and groups. From there, the doors are open—to connect, to communicate, to persuade.

Everyone's got a story. Every person, every organization. And just about everything we write—case studies, speeches, web copy, bios, marketing materials—can be improved by framing it in terms of story, or at least including story elements.

AN ACTOR AT WORK

Breathe Life into Your Case Studies

Case studies do not have to be boring. (Contrary to practically every one you've ever read.) Most case studies are unnecessarily dense in detail, self-centered where they should be reader-oriented, too general where they should be personal.

Imagine a case study that starts like this:

> *Richard Gilmore didn't need to check the computer readout to see that something on the production line was off. Nicknamed "Hawkeye" by his co-workers for his constant vigilance, the seventeen-year veteran could tell just by sight that the components were out of balance. After extensive study, the problem that Richard and his co-workers first spotted turned out to be a systemic failure in machine maintenance...*

Contrast that with the typical, "XYZ Company was experiencing quality control issues with one of its major engine systems. We conducted a study and found blah, blah, and blah. And furthermore, blah." Wouldn't you rather hear about Richard and find out how his story ends?

Of course you would. Because it's personal. And because it taps into the universal appeal of characters battling obstacles to achieve their goals. In short, it's a story.

Tell Your Story

Everyone needs to craft his or her own personal story. One that communicates who you are, as opposed to the things you do.

I was in a meeting recently where the participants went around the table introducing themselves. Most simply offered up a chronological listing of their employment history and various professional accomplishments, which they could have communicated less painfully by circulating their CVs.

How much more meaningful and memorable would it have been to say something like, "I went to school to become a teacher but thought it was impractical and pursued law instead. Now after twenty years in legal practice, here I am teaching." *Irony!*

Or: "I started out just answering phones. When things needed doing, I did them. I got interested in accounting, got a degree at the local community college, and now I'm finance manager." *Rags to riches!*

Or: "I was a high flyer on Wall Street, then I was indicted, imprisoned, and paroled. Now I'm a greeter at Walmart." *Fall from grace!*

Once you start thinking in story terms—about

characters and their struggles and about connecting cause and effect—you'll be better able to shape and communicate your own story.

Deliver a Winning Sales Pitch

For maximum credibility, let *others* tell your story. Customer testimonials, third-party endorsements, media coverage, industry rankings, and awards are always going to be more convincing and more meaningful than anything you say about yourself.

It's the reason we look to Zagat's or Yelp for restaurant recommendations or TripAdvisor for hotel reviews.

So step aside and let others do the selling.

SCENE 2
TAP INTO EMOTION

In acting, emotion is everything. The best actors can quickly, almost effortlessly, tap into a deep well of emotion and use it to connect meaningfully with the audience. In fact, for most good actors these reservoirs are never far from the surface.

(Which is partly why many actors have that volatile quality that makes them so entertaining—and dangerous— to be around sometimes.)

In business, "emotion" is a bit of a dirty word. Feelings are things to be guarded and held close. Excessive displays of emotion can earn you anything from a quizzical look to a referral to the company's Employee Assistance Program.

But emotion can be a supremely powerful tool with an unparalleled ability to break through to audiences, establish common ground, and win people over.

If you're uncomfortable with the concept, just call it "passion" or "conviction." However you label it, the judicious use of emotion can go a long way when you're facing disgruntled employees, skeptical media, or a hostile public.

COME OVER TO THE DARK SIDE

We saw in the Preview how a CEO used emotion to uplift and inspire. But sometimes a little anger—or at least a bit of well-directed righteous indignation—can be equally effective.

I remember watching the coverage of the attempt on Ronald Reagan's life. As with any crisis, the facts were sketchy in the early moments. Newscaster Frank Reynolds was on the desk for ABC.

At one point he conveyed a dramatic bulletin: Press Secretary James Brady was dead. Later, when the report turned out to be false, Reynolds became visibly agitated and barked to those off camera, "Let's get it nailed down...somebody...let's find out! Let's get it straight so we can report this thing accurately!"

It was a powerful moment. It demonstrated that in the midst of the chaos, someone was there who was absolutely adamant about getting the facts right. Reynolds was on our side and working like a bulldog to get us the truth.

In the first days of the BP oil spill, I kept wondering where the spokesman was who would say, "I am as frustrated as anybody. This is about peoples' lives and safety and livelihoods. This is our home, too. I feel awful about this and I'm going to do everything in my power to find an answer and make it right!"

A display of emotion that shows empathy and a little humanity can go a long way in situations like these.

AUTHENTICITY IS KEY

The most important thing about using emotion is to be genuine. Audiences can smell phoniness like animals can smell fear, so don't fake it. The great actors don't just try to *appear* angry or sad or joyous, they actually *feel* those emotions themselves.

I've watched friends in theater deliver such gut-wrenching performances that they're actually crying at the curtain call and are emotionally exhausted long after the lights go down.

So when using emotion, choose stories that really resonate with you. If you're truly present and in the moment, you shouldn't have to manufacture it.

AND DON'T OVERDO IT

It's also important to be sparing with emotion. If you go to the well too often, it loses its impact and people start to feel...squirmy.

Take John Boehner. He cries at the drop of a hat. Almost literally. I would hate to spill a glass of milk around that man.

Holding back a little, saving the big guns for when they're really needed, is a good idea. To illustrate, I'm afraid I'm going to have to talk about *Star Trek*, which I hope we can agree is the smartest and hottest thing a person can do.

As we all know, Spock is forever trying to suppress his human side. In "This Side of Paradise," Spock gets shot up with alien spores that turn him suddenly into this happy-go-lucky guy who laughs and cries and hangs upside down from tree branches and falls in love.

For most of us viewers it isn't a terribly pleasant experience. Gushy Spock is just a little too much to bear and we're mightily relieved when he's finally cured (thanks to Kirk ticking him off, as you'll recall).

In contrast, think about the ending of "Amok Time." This is the one where Spock is afflicted with Pon Farr, the Vulcan equivalent of spawning season. He finds himself in a battle with Kirk, his captain and best friend, and kills him.

Or so he thinks. Back on the *Enterprise*, we see coldly logical Spock announcing his intention to resign his commission and submit himself for court-martial where he'll surely be sentenced to death. Only then, Kirk suddenly appears—he wasn't dead after all! *(Thanks, Bones!)*

Spock spontaneously bursts out in joy, grabs his old friend by the shoulders and, with a great big smile, cries, "Jim!" He quickly gathers himself, thankfully, but it's that flash of emotion, rare and unexpected, that forever endears him to us.

Or at least to those of us who spent too many hours watching TV in our parents' basement.

CAN I BORROW A FEELING?

Great leaders have a natural talent for summoning the passions within themselves and their audiences.

But what if you're just not one of those types? Say you're more Spock than Kirk.

No matter how stiff or stoic we may feel, we all have something we're passionate about. Some emotional reservoir we can tap into and relate to our business.

SIX STEPS TO A BREAKTHROUGH

Here are a few ways to prime your emotional pump:

1 GET PERSONAL. Ask yourself some of the questions from the chapter on storytelling: What do you love about your job? What gets you excited and makes you proud? What does your family think about what you do? Have you had to make sacrifices to do the job well? These questions help us understand why we do what we do.

2 TALK ABOUT YOUR PASSIONS. Do you like art? Why exactly? Dig deep. Is it the beauty? The skill? The precision? The expression? Or if golf is your thing, what makes it so special? The discipline and focus required? The opportunity for continuous improvement? There are lessons to be drawn from your outside interests that can be applied to your business.

3 TALK ABOUT THE BUSINESS. Does your organization have a long history or distinctive heritage? What makes its products or services the best? Why are they loved by customers? Every organization has some touchstone that people can relate to. It can be pride in what you do, it can be history, it can be as simple as the bonds that develop between people who work together every day.

4 PAINT THE BIG PICTURE. Why is your company in business? To sell product? To make money for shareholders? There's got to be something more. Everyone wants to feel that what they do matters, that they're part of something bigger and more important than their everyday activities. Define that for the audience and celebrate it.

5 USE OTHERS' STORIES. Some people are uncomfortable talking about themselves (or they claim to be). In that case, find inspiring personal stories among employees or audience members that will resonate. Ronald Reagan popularized the practice of inviting everyday heroes to the State of the Union address, acknowledging them and telling their stories. Every president has done it since, because it usually works.

6 CELEBRATE HEROES. We all have our personal heroes. Who are yours? Nelson Mandela? Lech Walesa? Cal Ripkin? Lessons can be drawn from their struggles and achievements. Just be careful not to get carried away—few of us should be comparing our struggles to Gandhi's.

Those are just some of the ways to open yourself up and find a way to relate to your audience.

LIFT THEM UP, LET THEM IN

There's a reason facts are often described as "cold" and "hard"—they'll only get you so far.

Or, as author and marketing guru Seth Godin puts it: "The market is not seduced by logic. People are moved by stories and drama and hints and clues and discovery. Logic is a battering ram."

Emotion helps personalize the message and humanize the messenger. People want to see that side of you. By letting them in, you give them a reason to listen.

An Actor at Work

Nail a Job Interview

A proper display of emotion can be effective in a job interview. It has to be the right kind of emotion, of course. I wouldn't recommend rage or grief.

But excitement? Passion? Optimism? Eagerness? Those are all good things and can give your future employer a better sense of who you really are. Companies can find any number of people with the right qualifications, but ultimately they will choose someone who is interesting and fun and a good fit for their culture.

So prepare by asking yourself the kinds of questions from points 1 and 2 above. What do you love about your work? Who do you most admire and why? What's your life's goal? Then find a way to steer an answer or two toward those passions. Speak with conviction and energy and enthusiasm.

Deliver a More
Stirring Speech

When giving a speech, you have to invest every word and phrase with meaning. We've all had the experience while reading a book where you suddenly realize your mind has drifted off and you don't even know what you just read.

If you let this happen during a speech, you're dead in the water. The audience will recognize right away that you have checked out and then they will, too.

So you have to stay present at all times. It's not enough to *read* the words, you have to *feel* them. When you're talking about something joyful, you have to feel happy. If you're expressing frustration, show your irritation.

If you're talking about a person, picture that person in your head. If it's a process, visualize it, step by step, as you describe it. If it's an idea, paint a picture in your mind. Experience the words as you say them.

In a word, *act*.

SCENE 3
SHOW, DON'T TELL

hat if your speeches and PowerPoint presentations and web copy and videos could be as entertaining as the Hollywood blockbuster playing at your local multiplex? Or as meaningful as the indie film at your nearby art house cinema? Or as gripping as some of the best television dramas on your DVR?

Impossible? Probably.

Sorry, but let's face it—none of us are Steven Spielberg or Wes Anderson or David Chase.

But we could all do a little better, couldn't we? At least better than, say, the people behind *Harry and the Hendersons*?

One of the most important lessons from film and television and even theater is to show, don't tell.

Make Listening an Active Experience

Few of us like to be told things, to be spoon-fed information. Think of all those terrible movies or sitcoms where one character recaps all the action or explains what's just happened offscreen (as spoofed by the *Austin Powers* character Basil Exposition).

On the other hand, when we're shown instead of told, our minds have to work a little bit harder to put the pieces together. Suddenly we're engaged. Listening is no longer a passive exercise.

I talk elsewhere about cutting copy to the bare essentials (See "Slash and Burn"). But what if we used no words at all?

Silence Is Golden

David Mamet, in addition to being one of the most celebrated playwrights of the last couple of decades, also writes for film and television. In a wonderfully brutal and typically profane memo to his writers on the TV Show *The Unit*, Mamet advises them, among many other invaluable things, to "pretend the characters can't speak, and write a silent movie."

The result is a story told visually, through the actions and the expressiveness of the actors. I'm a big fan of shows like *Mad Men* and *Friday Night Lights*, known for using spare dialogue and long silences to great effect. It's amazing how much goes on, literally, between the lines.

As one of my instructors once said, "Actors express themselves through actions. That's why they're called actors, not talkers." See if you can find stories and images that are as expressive as Jon Hamm and Connie Britton.

Here's a fun exercise: try muting the volume on the TV and watch for a while in silence. You'll be surprised at how much of the content you understand without the sound. Sitcoms, soap operas, and, especially, commercials (because they have to work a little harder) are pretty easy to figure out. *That schlub's trying to get out of doing yard work. This guy's feeling super confident about his job interview. She's unnaturally excited about her new haircut.*

The point is, whatever and however you're communicating, words are just one tool to use—and often not the most important one.

THINK VISUALLY

An acting teacher once told me that the human mind can process eight hundred words a minute, but we can speak only three hundred. That's a pretty big potential attention gap. How are you going to fill it? Visually.

Look for ways to replace words with images. And make them really cool, surprising images, full of power and impact. Seth Godin wrote a sharp treatise called *Really Bad PowerPoint*, in which he gave this advice:

> Talking about pollution in Houston? Instead of giving me four bullet points of EPA data, why not read the stats but show me a photo of a bunch of dead birds, some smog and even a diseased lung?

Maybe a little too dramatic for some situations and corporate cultures, but that's the direction to go in. As Robert McKee said in *Story*, "Image is our first choice, dialogue the regretful second choice."

PAINT A VISUAL PICTURE

Don't just show pictures—create them in the minds of your audience. This is especially important when it comes to abstract or hard-to-grasp concepts. They can be meaningless without a vivid reference point.

Take really large numbers. Did you know Brazil is losing fifty thousand square miles of rain forest a year? Sounds like a lot, right? But how much is that, really? It's actually an area the size of Louisiana. Isn't that better? *

Here's an example I came across on TV's *The Amazing Race*. One leg of the competition took place in Dhaka, Bangladesh, which we're told is an incredibly dense city with one hundred thousand people per square mile. Once again, that sounds like a lot of people. But then our host, Phil, informs us that that's like cramming the entire population of the U.S. and Mexico into a space the size of Los Angeles. Very helpful, Phil!

And how far away is halfway to the moon anyway? I can barely grasp what all the way to the moon means. But tell me it's like five trips around the earth, or twenty round trips from New York to San Francisco, and I start to get it.

Make sure the visual pictures you conjure make sense to your audience.

QUICK QUIZ:
WHAT SPEAKS LOUDER THAN WORDS?

The best way to show is through action.

If you've ever spent some time on match.com or other dating sites, you'll find that ninety percent of the people there, when asked to describe themselves, do so literally. "I'm funny, intelligent, adventurous..." (Have you ever met anyone, by the way, who doesn't think he's funny or intelligent?)

Imagine how much more powerful those profiles would be if people actually demonstrated how funny and intelligent and adventurous they are. Think of it—instead of *saying* you're funny, *be* funny! Instead of saying you're intelligent, discuss the books you've read. Instead of saying you're adventurous, talk about that Class V white-water rafting trip you survived.

ACTION ILLUSTRATED

I was working with a law firm that wanted to attract new associate-level attorneys. A big selling point was the firm's culture—much more informal, laid-back, and fun than your typical stuffy law firm.

---

* *There's a really cool website called "Dimensions" where you can do this very thing— overlay big events and places on a map of your own neighborhood or an area you know. Go to howbigreally.com.*

But instead of announcing, as most would do, "Hey, we're the informal, laid-back, and fun firm," the attorneys put together a series of funny, quirky YouTube-style videos that included everything from commercial parodies to hallway beanbag fights.

The videos were a big hit and created a lot of industry buzz on blogs and message boards. Without ever saying that this was a different kind of firm, we demonstrated it.

The same law firm was celebrating its twenty-fifth anniversary. Though they're relatively small, they pride themselves on doing highly sophisticated legal work for blue-chip clients. Instead of competing with other firms their size, they choose to go up against the biggest firms.

So we put together a big, expensive book telling twenty-five stories from the firm's history. But the stories aren't about the firm, they're about the clients and the cool things those clients do. In fact, not a single attorney's name appears anywhere in the book. (Pretty much unprecedented for a law firm.)

The whole point was to show that they're playing in the big leagues. Or, in the words of an old advertising slogan, "Judge us by the company we keep." The book was hugely popular, won a couple of awards, and even helped bring in new business.

AN ACTOR AT WORK

Build a Better PowerPoint Presentation

Don't use the slides as your script. It's torture to watch someone read text off the screen with little additional embellishment. What's the point of having a speaker at all? You might as well just distribute printed handouts and save everyone the pain.

Keep words to a minimum. Find evocative visuals to convey your message. Scour the Internet. Pull stuff from YouTube. For inspiration, look to the entertainment industry, not your industry. (Just be careful not to run afoul of copyright laws and fair use standards—there are plenty of sources for free or inexpensive images.)

Create a More Striking Print Piece

Look for opportunities to replace text with pictures. I don't know whether a picture is still worth a thousand words, what with falling exchange rates and all, but it's worth a lot. Lean heavily on your graphic designer.

Be imaginative. Don't settle for the same old images everyone expects—the insurance industry umbrella or the diversity initiative's jigsaw puzzle or country quilt.

Speaking of insurance and creativity, those two concepts aren't necessarily mutually exclusive. I once did a photo shoot for a major national insurance company that was downright inspired. They put us in crazy wardrobe in front of bright, colorful backgrounds and gave us a funky array of props—everything from driftwood to toys to farm implements.

In one shot they had me posing in front of a pyramid of duct tape rolls while holding a fake duck in my arms. I asked the creative director what they could possibly use these pictures for and he said two things that were instructive.

First, he didn't know what specifically they'd be used for. They were creating a stock of images for future marketing materials. But he knew that whatever they created, the first priority was to engage the reader with provocative, surprising images.

Second, he said they were moving away from literal imagery and more toward suggestive and abstract visuals. Something to make readers think and leave them wanting to know more.

Beware of literalism. Keep your images simple and focused on a single good idea.

Produce a More Compelling Video

Some of the best documentaries have no narrator. Instead, they weave together a narrative with interviews, images, music, and maybe a few words on screen. So dump the narration.

It's harder, of course. It takes more time to film, because you have to elicit the right content from your interview subjects. And it takes more time to edit it all together seamlessly. But think of how much more powerful it could be.

And credible. Who is that corporate narrator supposed to be, anyway? What's she doing standing between the viewers and the content? And what's her agenda? Instead of having a narrator force-feed information to the audience, let the subjects speak for themselves—direct, unfiltered, and in their own words.

ACT

II II II II

PLAY TO YOUR AUDIENCE

"The audience is fifty percent of the performance."
—Shirley Booth, actor

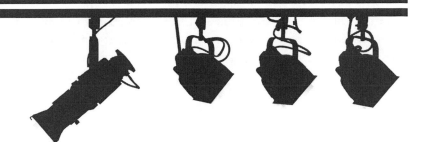

SCENE 4
LISTEN UP!

Mia Wallace: *"In conversation, do you listen or do you wait to talk?"*
Vincent Vega: *"I have to admit that I wait to talk,
but I'm trying harder to listen."*

—*PULP FICTION* *

istening is the most important skill in acting, communication, and probably life.

Everyone's heard this, everyone says they're a good listener, but how many people really put it into practice? Listening—truly listening—is hard work. And it doesn't always come naturally.

I'm as guilty of this as anyone. People in sales, marketing, and communications are absolutely fantastic talkers. Go to a happy hour and it's total conversational mayhem. Ideas flow like wine (and usually with it). People practically burst at the seams to share their thoughts. We're communicators; it's what we do. We love to talk, we love to be heard.

---

* *When searching for this quote I was surprised to learn that this scene was actually deleted from the theatrical version. I guess I've gotten used to the horribly edited TV version, which I imagine includes the scene because the networks had a huge hole to fill once they cut most of the movie's violence and profanity.*

But whatever your job is, listening is a vital skill for the success of both your communications and your career. It's the key to being tuned in to the needs of your audience and to understanding and getting along with others.

NOW HEAR THIS

Here are eight ways to be a better listener.

1 CONCENTRATE

Listening is critically important in improv. When you're on stage and your fellow ensemble members are constructing a richly detailed physical environment and establishing characters and relationships, you have to concentrate very hard to ensure you're not walking through an imaginary coffee table or hitting on your aunt.

We used to spend an insane amount of time in class on listening exercises. One of them involved passing objects from one person to another. Someone hands you a set of keys and you hand them to someone else, making sure you hand them off to the same person every time.

Sounds easy enough, right?

Try adding a second object, like a pen. Only the givers and receivers are different for this transaction. Still pretty manageable.

But then you bring in a notebook. And a hat. And a phone. And a scarf. Pretty soon you're juggling more than a half-dozen objects. And you have to keep it up for ten or fifteen minutes without pausing or interrupting the flow.

Exhausted? Good. That means you're listening.

2 BUT ALSO RELAX

As an actor, I do print shoots where I might have my picture taken three hundred or more times in an hour or two. And every pose is a little different, with constant direction and tweaking from the photographer: "Give me an open-mouthed smile. Now closemouthed. Angle your body forty-five degrees. Now face straight to camera. Look serious. Turn to the right. Tilt your head. Chin up. Slide to the left a half step. One more inch. Cross your arms. No, other way."

And so on and so on. After a while you just learn to relax and listen and do as you're told. It's almost Zen-like. And it's a great exercise in truly listening.

On the other hand, I have a Pilates instructor who runs us through a precise, consistent regimen every class. After a couple of years, I've grown really accustomed to it, to the point where I find I'm no longer really listening. She'll occasionally shake things up and go "off script," adding a move or switching the order, and suddenly I'm out of sync with the class.

Listening is about letting go and listening to the actual words people are speaking, not the words we expect to hear.

3 BE PATIENT

It's also a matter of patience and discipline. I know a guy who sits down once a week with a friend for an hour. In the first half hour, one of them talks and the other one listens. Just listens. No interruptions, no questions, no affirmations, nothing. Then they switch roles.

I can't imagine holding my tongue like that for thirty minutes. It's hard not to take on the role of fixer or problem-solver. But sometimes people just need to be heard, and shutting up can be more valuable than anything we might have to say. Which brings us to interrupters and sentence-finishers.

4 STOP INTERRUPTING

Many people pride themselves on being smart and understanding and intuitive. Anticipating needs, analyzing a situation, cutting to the chase—these skills are essential to business.

But they can sometimes manifest themselves in the annoying

habit of finishing peoples' sentences for them. It's not only rude, but even if you have a pretty good batting average when it comes to guessing peoples' thoughts, you're going to be wrong enough times to make interrupting a bad idea.

5 LISTEN BEYOND THE WORDS

Before I started acting I didn't really understand what it meant to "listen" in that context. People are reciting scripted lines, right? What's there to listen to? They say their lines, you say yours, repeat.

But there are hundreds of ways to say, "I could kill you"—angrily, seductively, facetiously. And it can be very helpful to know whether you're being threatened, seduced, or kidded. It's not just the words; you have to listen for the intention behind them.

Do yourself a favor: Google the video for "Don Draper says what." You'll be amazed at how many different meanings can be expressed by one simple word.

6 DON'T ASSUME

Most business people claim to be closely attuned to the needs and wants of their customers and employees. But they're often working on outdated information or knee-jerk assumptions.

Often, an executive will assure me that he's got his finger on the proverbial pulse of his audience. But when you interview those people you find a huge disconnect between their concerns and his assumptions.

A big part of listening involves questioning. Followed by, um, *listening*.

7 BE PERSISTENT

Listening also requires persistence. Because people sometimes don't do a very good job of expressing themselves. Or they don't know what they want. Or what they want changes over time.

I know a lawyer who frequently deposes witnesses. It's amazing, he says, how even the "friendly" ones tend to mix up their facts, change their stories and shade the truth a little.

He finds he has to frequently check back, verify, and adjust accordingly.

8 BE BRAVE

Sometimes we don't listen because we don't bother to ask. And we don't ask because we don't want to hear the answer—sort of the corporate version of "don't ask, don't tell."

I used to work with a very demanding person. Staff meetings were akin to the Spanish Inquisition. (And, contrary to what we learned from Monty Python, this was one time *everybody* expected the Spanish Inquisition.)

So people would gloss over things, cover up mistakes, or fail to disclose when a project was going off course. That almost always backfired, and the consequences were inevitably worse than if we had just been up-front in the first place.

Or, to get back to *Pulp Fiction*, maybe we were taking our cue from Jules, who said, "If my answers frighten you then you should cease asking scary questions." Bad advice.

WAIT, WHAT ABOUT BODY LANGUAGE?

Some may note a conspicuous absence from this discussion of any mention of body language. There's no shortage of information on the topic, and I don't claim to be an expert.

In fact, I'm a bit of a body language renegade. I've been known to occasionally put my hands in my pockets when speaking to a group and to cross my leg away from the person I'm having a conversation with.

And like a cigar is sometimes just a cigar, sometimes an itch is just an itch. And a pair of arms crossed in front of the chest could simply mean a person's cold.

Clearly there's something to it, but I'm going to assume that you're fairly intuitive and don't need to be told that "a harsh or blank expression often indicates outright hostility," as one expert explains.

ZEN AND THE ART OF LISTENING

In yoga, the instructors tell you that it's all about tuning out the distractions of the day and noises in your head and just listening to your body. (My body's usually saying "ouch.") I haven't gotten to that point where I can totally clear my head and I don't know if I ever will.

But I have found those moments where listening is a truly active, engaging, and focused experience. It may never be as fun for me as talking, but it definitely has its rewards.

AN ACTOR AT WORK

Be a Better Boss

If ever there was a time to put down the BlackBerry and back away from the computer screen, it's when employees come to you for help or with questions. This can be an intimidating experience for some people, so the least you can do is give them your full attention.

If you appear distracted or impatient, they're not going to express themselves clearly or fully. So put down your stuff, look them in the eye, and really listen.

And when you've answered the question, ask if they feel you've answered it. Watch what they say and how they say it. Don't let them leave until you've really resolved the situation.

I once worked with a woman who had a habit of throwing up her arms in exasperation and snapping, "What!?" whenever someone came to her with a question or request. True "service with a snarl." It wasn't long before people just started going around her and leaving her out of the loop.

In retrospect, maybe that was her goal all along! But signaling a readiness to listen by having an open door and an open mind is a better strategy over the long run.

Deal Successfully with the Media

When speaking with reporters, be sure to listen carefully and stick to the questions that are asked. This is especially important when you're involved in a controversial issue or find yourself in a confrontational situation.

Stick to the topic at hand. Don't anticipate what they're asking and interrupt. Wait to hear what they actually say before you answer. This is not the time to demonstrate your Amazing Kreskin-like predictive powers.

And when you get to the end of your answer, *stop talking*. A favorite tactic of reporters is to exploit the awkward pause. You'll come to the end of your answer and they won't say anything. The natural instinct for most humans is to fill the uncomfortable void by jabbering away, which reporters are all too happy to let you do. That's usually where the most priceless—and quotable—blunders occur.

Resist the urge. Embrace the silence. Be complete, be courteous, be helpful. But most of all, be careful.

Be More Responsive

The ultimate manifestation of listening is to actually follow through on what you hear. So if someone provides edits to a document, incorporate them, or explain why you didn't. If an employee or reporter poses a question you can't answer, make sure you follow up later with the information. If your boss asks you to do something, do it.

You'll be surprised at what a positive impact this can have. Most people have grown so accustomed to not being heard that they'll be blown away by your responsiveness. It's a sad commentary that the simple act of following up can stand out so starkly, but it does.

Regrettably, many people are weasels. Don't be one.

Interact with an Audience

Always build time into your presentation for questions and discussion. That's often where the most valuable and most targeted content comes from.

When someone asks a question, repeat it or rephrase it so others can hear it and so you can be sure you've understood it. Encourage the questioner to correct you if you got it wrong and confirm at the end whether your answer is satisfactory.

But don't get too carried away—if you can't nail it after a couple of tries, arrange to talk individually afterwards.

SCENE 5

CONNECT AND PROJECT

n the seminal actors' text *Audition*, Michael Shurtleff talks about "the moment before":

> Every scene you will ever act begins in the middle...[t]his is true if you do a scene at the beginning of a play or in the middle of a play or the end of the play. Something always precedes what you are doing.

So prior to entering a scene, the actor works to put what's to come into the context of everything that's come before—the character's history and emotional state and relationship with the other characters.

The moment before is crucial to grounding the performance in the reality of the production, and thus connecting with the audience.

The same lesson applies to business. Before approaching any communication, think about where it fits in the overall context of what your audience knows, what they have heard, and what they expect. Then use that knowledge to connect with them.

CREATE A PROFILE

Whether it's a speech, internal memo, web copy, or marketing piece, you must first put yourself in your audience's shoes. It doesn't matter whether you are talking to hundreds of people or just one; an audience is an audience.

Ideally, you will have research at your disposal—surveys, focus groups, even anecdotal findings that can help you better understand them.

Absent that (or even in addition to it), you can create a profile. Here are some questions to ask to determine where they are in the story you're telling.

- Who are they?
- What do they want?
- What do they know about us?
- What are their perceptions of me/the organization/ our product or services?
- What are their misperceptions?
- What are their doubts?
- What are their fears?
- What are their beliefs?
- What do they expect?
- What is their mood? Are they:
  - Confident?
  - Complacent?
  - Hopeful?
  - Anxious?

- ☐ Skeptical?
- ☐ Distrustful?
- ☐ Disappointed?
- ☐ Fearful?
- ☐ Angry?
- ☐ Combative?
- ■ What inspires them?
- ■ What are they proud of?
- ■ What brings them together?
- ■ What do we have in common?

That's the starting point. Without knowing these things, any communication will be tone-deaf. Without addressing the audience's concerns, you'll never get them to listen.

SHINE A LIGHT

The mood of an audience can range from welcoming to hostile, from confident to distrustful.

There's an old adage, "Hang a lantern on your problems." That is, if you've got a weakness or vulnerability, you should be the first to call it out. That way, you can explain it and get your side of the story across first. When you hide or avoid an issue, you look like you're guilty of something.

Much of the corporate world adheres to the crazy idea that we should never dwell on the negative. We should turn—twist, even—everything into a positive statement. I always prefer to address any negative perceptions directly and right up front.

If the audience is disappointed in the company's performance and doesn't think management is doing anything about it, start by saying, "I know you're disappointed in our performance. So are we. Let me tell you what we're doing about it."

It's such a ridiculously simple technique. By acknowledging their concerns you show you understand and that you're listening.

But too often the temptation is to begin with corporate boilerplate or rosy scenarios that cause everyone reading or watching to immediately tune out and dismiss you as out of touch and irrelevant.

It's not necessary to go through a whole laundry list of problems right at the top. But by addressing one or two of the main ones, you'll gain a measure of credibility. Tackling the others as you go along helps sustain it.

PLAY TO THE BALCONY

In theater, everything has to be a little larger than life. Bigger gestures, bolder movement, louder voice. Mike Myers tells a story from his childhood about his mother, a trained actress herself, egging him on at auditions. "Eyes and teeth!" she'd say.

It's called "projecting" or "playing to the balcony," and it's the theater equivalent of "swinging for the fences." Go big or go home.

In communications you have three goals: inform, motivate, and activate. Most communications begin and end with only the first one. But conveying information is the absolute least we can demand of communication. If we were to set up a pyramid for communications similar to Maslow's hierarchy of needs, information would be down at the base, like food, shelter, and breathing.

After all, why do we go to the movies? Is it to get caught up in a story and connect with the characters and be transported to another time and place? Or is to get information?

There's so much more you can do than simply pass along data. Especially if you've gone to all the trouble of getting to understand your audience and their concerns. Armed with that insight, you can develop communications that are relevant and that "echo off the back wall," as actors learn to do in projecting their voices.

THREE LITTLE QUESTIONS

In order to inform, motivate, and activate, your communications should answer these three questions:

1 WHAT DO YOU WANT THE AUDIENCE TO KNOW?

2 WHAT DO YOU WANT THEM TO FEEL?

3 WHAT DO YOU WANT THEM TO DO?

Number 1 is easy. It's the basics: the information, the content, the stuff you want to convey. But it's not enough to just give them the facts. If you want the information to stick, you have to grab their hearts.

So what do you want them to feel? Inspired? Comforted? Proud? Challenged? Eager? Figure out the words, images, and stories that will accomplish that. If you've done your research or created an audience profile, this shouldn't be guesswork.

The final step is to turn those feelings into actions. It's not enough to influence opinions; you want to change behaviors. What do you want your audience to *do*?

Buy your product? Check out your website? "Like" your page on Facebook? Do you want employees to cut costs? Work better as a team? Find new customers?

Whatever it is you want them to do, it must be specific. "Improve quality" doesn't help anyone. "Strive for an error rate of less than one-tenth of one percent" does.

ONE FINAL QUESTION

Ultimately, the number one concern on every person's mind is, "What's in it for me?" That's what it all comes down to, and it's the fundamental question you must answer in every communication.

Go on any corporate website and you'll see long lists of product features and service descriptions. It's all inward-facing. Instead of "we do this" and "we offer that," turn your communications outward. What are the major challenges your customers face and how do you solve their problems?

Encore!

Every once in a while on stage you experience this magical moment of intense connection with the audience. You may not be able to see past the glare of the spotlights, but you can sense they're there with you, moving and feeling and even breathing as one.

Through words and expression you've managed to bridge that gap—capturing their hopes and aspirations, giving voice to their fears and insecurities, embodying the very nature of what it means to be alive, to be human.

And it doesn't just happen by chance. It's the essence of what playwrights and actors do. It's strategic.

We can do the same in business by finding that place where our own goals and priorities intersect with and address our audience's interests and needs. Without that connection, your time on the stage will be meaningless and ineffective. All "sound and fury, signifying nothing."

An Actor at Work

Apply for a Job

When you're writing to someone for a job or preparing for an interview, there's no reason these days for that person to be a stranger.

Before your interview, go online and find out as much as you can about the person you're going to see. Google her. Google her company. Look up her bio on the company's website. Check out her work history on LinkedIn. Make sure you know as much as you can about your interviewer and the company you want to work for.

Having personal knowledge about your interviewer—where she went to school, what her responsibilities are, her interests and hobbies and goals and priorities—is incredibly useful for making a connection.

And with LinkedIn, you may even find that someone you know knows her, too. Use your contacts to find out everything you can and even to help make an introduction.

Counsel an Employee More Effectively

Sometimes you'll hear managers say, "I treat everyone the same." That can be a fatal mistake.

Of course you want to treat people equitably and fairly. You don't want to create and apply different standards. But you do need to treat people differently.

Some people are motivated by financial rewards. Others by the prestige of a corner office. Some want to be given a visible leadership role. Others respond to awards.

When you're working with an employee on a performance issue, think ahead about the kind of person he is. That's your audience. Know his wants, his needs, his personality, how he reacts under stress, how confident he is, whether he needs reassurance or inspiration or responds well to a figurative kick in the pants.

All of these things and more are important. Tailor your communication to the individual.

Withstand a Siege

Say your organization is the subject of an unflattering news story, pessimistic analyst report, or protest from the community. How do you handle your internal audience of employees?

Inform them. Don't bother trying to hide the news—they already know or soon will. This is your chance to put the story in context, correct any errors, and give them all the facts.

Motivate them by explaining the big picture. Remind them of the things that make the organization great. Show them that you're prepared to fight, if necessary, for the organization's reputation. Assure them that this, too, shall pass.

Finally, activate them—enlist them in the effort to set the record straight. Arm them with talking points and Q&A. Encourage them to spread the word to their associates, customers, friends, and neighbors. Provide templates for them to use in writing letters to the editor or blog posts.

Adjust a Presentation on the Fly

Did you know Martin Luther King Jr. performed much of his "I Have a Dream" speech off the cuff?

He actually started a different speech that day, one that he and his advisors had worked on for weeks. But one of those advisors, Mahalia Jackson, didn't like the direction the Reverend was going. She called out, "Tell 'em about the dream, Martin!"

After pausing to collect himself, King tossed aside his prepared speech and proceeded to wing it. Calling up themes from earlier sermons, he wove together one of modern history's great pieces of rhetoric.

Okay, that's a tough standard to live up to, but the lesson still applies. If you sense you're losing your audience, be prepared to shake things up. Cut your material, shift things around, tell a story, improvise.

Or ask a question. Take one of the points from your material and ask if anyone has had a related experience. Get them to share it. Start a conversation and keep it moving.

The worst thing you can do is ignore your audience's indifference and stick rigidly to your prepared remarks.

SCENE 6

HIS MASTER'S VOICE

common feature of poorly written dialogue in films and plays is that all the characters sound the same. Same style, same syntax, same word choice. It's not individual voices we hear; it's the voice of the writer.

The same thing happens every day in business. People are afraid to let their personalities shine through. Everything is standardized and formalized and sterilized—scrubbed free of the individual traits and quirks that make us human.

Playing to your audience goes beyond discerning their needs and determining what to say. It also involves speaking to them in a voice that is recognizable as authentic and true.

People want to hear the real you, the everyday you. Much of this book is about helping you find and express your own voice, and you'll find lots of practical tips in chapters like "Plainly Speaking" and "Tap Into Emotion."

The really tricky thing is capturing someone else's voice.

Channeling Others

Sometimes we have to write for or with other people, and it's not always easy. But we have a leg up on the screenwriter: the characters we write for are real.

Whether you're penning an article under someone else's name or a speech for another person, capturing the voice of the speaker is critical to making the communication sound natural and authentic. (It also goes a long way toward getting it approved by that person— *"Hey, nice job! Sounds just like me!"*)

By his own admission, George W. Bush was no master orator. But he unquestionably had a distinctive voice, and his speechwriters managed to capture it successfully. But not everyone we write for will have such a strong personal style.

So how do you go about capturing someone's voice? For some people it just comes naturally. They sit down, have a conversation, read a speech or article or two, and quickly grasp the other person's style. It's like having an ear for dialogue.

I used to spend a lot of time writing for a particular CEO. I really got inside his head, to the point that I was writing his personal verbal tics into his speeches. He had to tell me to stop using the phrase, "Okay, guys," because it was a habit he was trying to break.

(And I recognize that "okay, guys" isn't exactly soaring rhetoric, but it was his voice, not mine.)

When it's not coming naturally, there are a variety of ways to approach the problem. But if you're just putting words in someone else's mouth, it's never going to ring true. The words you choose and the way you use them should be familiar and recognizable as their own—to them and their audience.

BROADLY SPEAKING

This concept isn't limited to individuals, by the way. Organizations have a voice, too. Some are articulated better than others and some are purely unintentional, but all companies have one.

So just as every person has a distinctive verbal pattern and rhythm and vocabulary, every organization has a certain tone and culture that's reflected—or should be reflected—in its online presence, marketing materials, and other things.

AN ACTOR AT WORK

Ghostwrite a Speech or Other Document

Whether you're writing for a colleague or a stranger (such as a board member or a guest at an industry conference), your first step is to use as many of her words as possible. Talk to her and find out what she wants to say.

Next, review any of her existing speeches, memos or other writing. Transcripts are good; video is even better. Try to answer these questions:

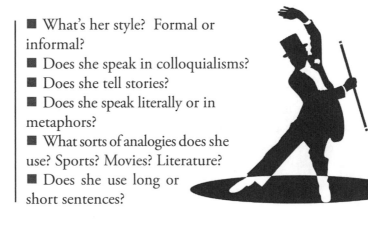

- What's her style? Formal or informal?
- Does she speak in colloquialisms?
- Does she tell stories?
- Does she speak literally or in metaphors?
- What sorts of analogies does she use? Sports? Movies? Literature?
- Does she use long or short sentences?

- What kind of words does she choose?
- What are some common phrases that keep coming up?
- Is there a rhythm? A tempo?
- What is her mood? What's the audience's mood?
- Does she communicate like a coach? A professor? A neighbor?

Finally, accompany her if you can when she's speaking somewhere. Unscripted occasions, like Q&A sessions, are especially helpful, since she'll likely be speaking in her natural, everyday vernacular.

Ultimately it will come to you. Maybe not right away, but after spending some time in that person's head and world.

Give Your Website an Authenticity Audit

Your website has a voice, and it's speaking directly to your customers, members, and the public.

Make sure it says what you want it to say. Look at the design, the words, the colors, the tone. Then think about these questions and how they match your organization's culture and brand. Is the site:

- Flashy with cool graphics, or simple and straightforward?
- Inviting and friendly, or designed to impress?
- Human-scaled or institutional?
- Intellectual or emotional?
- Artistic or practical?
- Grounded or dreamy?
- Wordy or visual?

- Detailed or minimalist?
- Colorful or stark?
- Warm or cool?
- Quiet or loud?

These are the kinds of questions you can and should ask about anything that represents your organization, from your marketing materials to your office furnishings. It all says something.

ACT

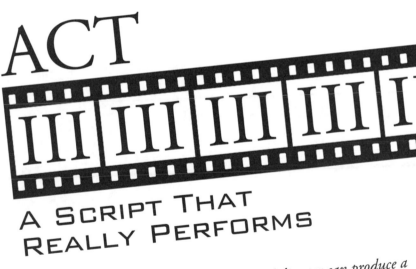

III III III III I

A SCRIPT THAT
REALLY PERFORMS

"With a good script, a good director can produce a masterpiece. With the same script, a mediocre director can produce a passable film. But with a bad script even a good director can't possibly make a good film."
—Akira Kurosawa, film director

SCENE 7
LANGUAGE MATTERS

e all have our favorite movies. I have probably watched the first two *Godfather* films more than twenty times each.

Why do we go back and watch the same movie over and over? Because we like it, obviously. Maybe because it's familiar. Or perhaps it "says something" to us.

But one big reason we might watch a movie or read a book multiple times is because, while that film or book never changes, our reaction to it does. Because we're different when we see it again. We've accumulated new life experiences and points of view.

Language does this, too. The words may stay the same, but their meaning is fluid—from person to person, across cultures, and over time. As the Italian poet Antonio Porchia put it:

> **"** What words say does not last.
> The words last. Because words
> are always the same, and what they
> say is never the same.
>
> —From *Voces*, English translation by W.S. Merwin

At the core of every communication is the written word. How we choose and use our words carries tremendous potential for success or failure.

BE HONEST

A long time ago I read a Hemingway quote that had a big impact on my writing: "All you have to do is write one true sentence. Write the truest sentence that you know."

What he meant by "true" can be interpreted any number of ways, I'm sure. Factually accurate, of course. But to me it's always meant that you can stand behind each and every sentence you write. It's authentic, BS-free, unpretentious, and devoid of cliché.

When I'm performing in a show, I'm actually more nervous when friends or family are in the audience. I think it's because the people who know us best can see right through our everyday parlor tricks, contrivances, bluffs, and boasts. They keep us honest.

When you're writing, think of the people you're closest to—best friends, family members, a spouse. How would you write if you knew they were going to read it?

BE PRECISE

My first boss out of college was a lawyer, not a communications person. He would cross-examine my every word. It was painful and aggravating. But over time, he helped break me of many of the bad writing habits I developed in college.

Like flabby over-writing and long, lazy sentences borne of minimum page counts. Highfalutin' language that serves little purpose other than to show off your SAT vocabulary. And imprecise word choice that gets overlooked in the stew of ideas. These habits become ingrained in school because they're very often rewarded.

And it's not just the undergrads who are the problem. The *Wall Street Journal* recently reported that business schools are beefing up their writing programs in response to employer complaints:

> **"** While MBA students'
> quantitative skills are
> prized by employers, their writing
> and presentation skills have been
> a perennial complaint. Employers
> and writing coaches say business-
> school graduates tend to ramble,
> use pretentious vocabulary or pen
> too-casual emails.

So I was taught, under the sharp point of the red editing pen of that first boss, that every single word has to have a purpose. Every. Single. Word.

But Also Be Vague When Necessary

Young writers tend to speak in absolutes, partly because passion and metaphysical certainty about the world just go hand in hand with youth. But also because the college thesis generally demands bold hypotheses and brash claims.

But business, like life, is rarely black and white. Assertions often require qualifiers: usually, sometimes, reportedly, purportedly, generally.

What do I mean by that? Look at the previous two paragraphs. There's a qualifier in every sentence: tend to, partly, generally, rarely and often.

Vagueness can be carried to an extreme, of course. Where an assertion is true, you should make it. Most business writing suffers from the lack of a strong point of view. That's right—I feel confident enough to say most.

BEWARE OF LOADED WORDS

People interpret language though the prism of their own personal experiences and biases, and certain words will trigger a negative reaction.

Politics is full of loaded words, and the rhetorical ground is constantly shifting to accommodate changing sensibilities. Back in the early days of the republic, the Defense Department was called the War Department. In the '80s, "affirmative action" gave way to "equal opportunity." And hardly anyone says "welfare" anymore—and if they do, it's likely they've got a specific ax to grind.

But plenty of other everyday words come loaded with extra baggage. "Allegedly" and "supposedly" can unnecessarily cast suspicion, whereas "reportedly" and "apparently" are more neutral and benign. Beware of the word "only," as in, "Is this your *only* job?" *(Slacker!)* Try "sole" instead. And everyone who's had the temerity to go to dinner alone has heard the unwelcome greeting, "Is it *just* you tonight?" *(Pathetic and lonely you!)*

Cultural differences can also load words with unexpected volatility. Try calling your next plan a "scheme," as the British do, and see how many eyebrows you raise.

Scour your writing and avoid those words that can provoke a reaction that prejudices the reader and distracts from what you're trying to communicate.

AVOID THE NEGATIVE

That same first boss of mine once said, "'Unfortunately' is an unfortunate way to begin a sentence." Cute, huh? I can't even say the word today without flinching. Certainly it's a perfectly serviceable word that has its merits. But it's also a negative word, and should be used with caution.

The same goes for "but." You can often substitute "and" for "but," as in, "We lost our funding, ~~but~~ and we're exploring other sources of revenue." It's subtle, but there's a difference. "But" can carry a negative, defeatist connotation. "And" moves past the negative and toward a solution.

Please note that this is not a prescription for papering over bad news with obvious BS, such as, "Recent events have afforded us an exciting opportunity to engage fresh sources of alternative funding!"

MAKE THE MOST OF POWER WORDS

In the screenwriting manual *Story*, Robert McKee discusses the suspense sentence:

> **"** In ill-written dialogue useless words, especially prepositional phrases, float to the ends of sentences. Consequently, meaning sits somewhere in the middle...Excellent film dialogue tends to shape itself into the periodic sentence: 'If you didn't want me to do it, why'd you give me that...' Look? Gun? Kiss? The periodic sentence is the 'suspense sentence.' Its meaning is delayed until the very last word, forcing both the actor and audience to listen to the end of the line.

McKee's advice can be applied to speeches, presentations, and videos, but it's also useful in other settings, like social media. (Twitter and Facebook posts are bits of an ongoing conversation, so your most powerful words and ideas should land at the end of the message, like a comic's punch line.)

What's more effective?

```
We will all lose our jobs if we
don't cut costs.
```

or

```
If we don't cut costs we will all
lose our jobs.
```

```
Learn how our latest offering will
change your business forever at our
upcoming seminar.
```

or

```
Come to our seminar and learn how
our latest offering will change
your business forever.
```

```
Tomorrow we shall die, so eat, drink
and be merry.
```

or

```
Eat, drink and be merry, for tomorrow
we shall die.
```

Once you become aware of this you'll never be able to listen to a speech or enjoy TV in the same way again.

RECOGNIZE YOUR "CRUTCH" WORDS

We all have our verbal tics—words and phrases we use all the time. These may be relatively benign, "go-to" words that we simply prefer to use. Or they may be "crutches"—words we've become overly reliant on.

I'm not talking about the widely overused ones like "basically," or the frequently misused ones, like "frankly" (which should be reserved for surprising revelations, not predictable viewpoints like "Frankly, I don't enjoy root canal").

I'm talking about the personal patterns each of us exhibits. It's good to get a handle on this, lest we become repetitive and predictable. A great tool for revealing those crutch words is the "word cloud." If you don't know, a word cloud is a fun little app that analyzes any document and sizes the words in proportion to their use.

There are lots of places on the web where you can generate word clouds. One is Wordle.net. When I wordled this book, here's what I got:

Fascinating. I'm glad that some of the most frequently used words include "people," "words," "communications," "audience," "story," and "writing." But look at some of the other big ones: "just" (sounds defensive), "really" (am I trying too hard to persuade?), and "like" (does that signal an over-reliance on similes and analogies?).

What about the prevalence of "good" and "things?" Do they signify an elegant simplicity or a lack of creativity? And, after I just preached about the importance of qualifiers, the irony of "always" appearing fairly prominently in the cloud is not lost on me.

It's hard to say what these findings mean, and we can drive ourselves crazy over-analyzing them, but I think it's good (there I go again) food for thought. There's nothing wrong with a little self-awareness.

BE POETIC

I had another boss who would occasionally come into my office with a letter or other document she had written and ask me to "make it sing." Up to then I wasn't aware I had this special skill, but it became something of a joke around the office, with people requesting that I make their phone messages, calendar entries, and lunch orders sing.

It was an interesting word choice. I've forever regretted my almost total lack of musical instinct or talent, yet I am somehow tuned in to the music of language—its shape and contours and rhythms.

Don't be afraid to make your prose poetic at times. Speeches, marketing copy, and e-mails can sometimes benefit from a little alliteration. Or the occasional rhythm or rhyme. (See what I did there?)

Just be careful. It's got to be done well. And it's got to be done for a purpose, whether playful or inspirational. Otherwise it's distracting.

I love reading and listening to great speeches. One of my favorites is Rev. Jesse Jackson's 1988 speech to the Democratic National Convention. It's one inspiring piece of rhetoric. Here's a sample:

> **"**I was born in the slum, but the slum was not born in me. And it wasn't born in you, and you can make it. Wherever you are tonight, you can make it. Hold your head high; stick your chest out. You can make it. It gets dark sometimes, but the morning comes. Don't you surrender! Suffering breeds character, character breeds faith. In the end faith will not disappoint.

So be inspired. And when the time and place is right, let your own words soar.

Words have consequences. They carry tremendous weight. Choose them wisely.

 Language exerts hidden power, like the moon on the tides.
—RITA MAE BROWN, NOVELIST

 Nothing exists except through language.
—HANS-GEORG GADAMER, PHILOSOPHER

AN ACTOR AT WORK

Prepare a Speech That Really Delivers

Spoken language is very different from written language. So if you're preparing a speech, be sure to read it aloud in advance.

I have been in countless rehearsals for business conferences where it's clear that the speaker is reading the speech for the very first time. No matter how many times you read it to yourself, there are things you'll never pick up until you've read it in the form it will ultimately take: out loud.

When you do, you'll find sentences that are too long to say in one breath. Paragraphs that put you to sleep. Proper names you can't pronounce. Tongue twisters.

Don't wait until the last minute—read it early, read it often, read it out loud.

Leave a Better Voice Mail

Beyond the words you choose, be mindful of how you use them. Tone is an important element of language.

Leaving a voice mail is like delivering a mini-speech, though it's usually unscripted and unrehearsed. And because it's a one-way communication, you're unable to judge in real time how your audience perceives it and adjust accordingly. As a result, a voice mail message carries tremendous potential for misinterpretation.

Obviously, you should plan what you're going to say so your message is focused and concise. And you should avoid leaving a voice mail when you're angry or really stressed. But you should also think hard about how your words and tone of voice could be interpreted.

I was told by a couple of people that I sometimes sound irritated or angry on voice mail. It was a real revelation. I thought my delivery was simply brisk and straightforward. Then a colleague gave me a great idea: she told me to smile when I leave a message. It was such a simple solution—it's hard to sound angry when you're smiling.

So be careful with voice mail. Put yourself in the listener's shoes. And if it's a really difficult message that takes a lot of planning and practice? That's probably a sign that you should choose a different vehicle than voice mail.

Use E-mail Wisely

E-mail is tough. It's not an ideal medium for subtlety and nuance. Sarcasm doesn't come across well, and even humor has its hazards.

If you don't know the person you're e-mailing very well, be careful. If you have to load your message up with smiley or winky emoticons, that's a sign that what you're trying to convey is too complex for written words.

Pick up the phone instead. Or go see him in person.

SCENE 8

PLAINLY SPEAKING

"I would never use a long word where a short one would answer the purpose. I know there are professors in this country who 'ligate' arteries. Other surgeons only tie them, and it stops the bleeding just as well."

—OLIVER WENDELL HOLMES

I n the old days of acting, the style was formal and presentational. Think Laurence Olivier stepping to the lip of the stage to deliver a soliloquy. Or watch any black-and-white melodrama from the forties or fifties.

As the years go by, this style has become more and more jarring to contemporary sensibilities, where we're all encouraged to be "real." What broke it all open was a method of acting and a generation of actors like Marlon Brando and James Dean and, later, Robert DeNiro and Al Pacino, among many others, who overturned convention and brought a then-startling realism to their performances. They'd mumble, stumble, and toss off their lines like they were making them up on the spot (which, in some cases, they were).

Much the same was happening in art and music and literature—people defying formal structures and tearing down old institutions and ways of doing things. In the twentieth century, Hemingway embodied this stripped-down simplicity. In the short story *Fathers and Sons*, the main character, speaking achingly of the past, says simply, "Long time ago good; now no good." Imagine Henry James or Nathaniel Hawthorne writing that.

TALK LIKE REAL PEOPLE

This drive toward simplicity and naturalism comes up constantly. In commercial acting you're directed to recite the lines as if you were talking one-on-one with a friend.

Actor Michael Caine has said that one of the highest compliments you can give an actor is to mistakenly interrupt him when he's practicing lines with another actor. Acting, when it's done well, should appear as natural and authentic as a normal conversation.

More and more businesses are getting the message, and communicating like real people do. But empty terms like world-class, value-added, synergy, optimized, and just about any phrase with the word "solution" in it persist.

FEAR AND LOATHING IN THE BOARDROOM

For a very short time I had a small law firm as a client. It started well. They said they were different from other firms, and they wanted their website to reflect that. So we talked to the partners and to the clients and found they did, indeed, have a refreshing approach to doing business. We developed messages and web copy to reflect that—simple, informal, conversational.

But the older partners grew increasingly uncomfortable with this new direction. I should have seen it coming, because they also weren't convinced they even needed a website at all! Over time they beat the copy into submission, stretching out the sentences and adding endless adjectives and hollow buzzwords.

We ultimately had to part ways when one of them advised me to go on their competitors' websites and pull ideas and even language from there. (These weren't intellectual property lawyers, obviously.)

In the end, they did not want to stand out. They feared looking weird. They sought the security of being like everyone else.

Serious Business

When these debates come up, there are always those who argue that an informal approach is wholly inappropriate for "serious" firms, like those in technology or consulting or the law. They say that when businesses are talking to other businesses, the rules are different—industry jargon is expected and serves as useful shorthand among insiders.

Granted, it's true that a medical device manufacturer is going to communicate differently than a cupcake baker. But overused words and phrases like "best practice" and "full-service" have become so commonplace they could mean practically anything and, as a consequence, mean almost nothing.

Every company is capable of moving the needle toward writing that is more human in scale and tone. After all, customers are ultimately people, right?

You Say Tomato,
They Say *Solanum lycopersicum*

It's not just the technical people like engineers and scientists who tend to rely heavily on inside jargon, buzzwords and acronyms. Even professional communicators—the people charged with translating all this nonsense into "humanspeak"—can get caught up in this way of communicating (or, more accurately, *not* communicating).

It's understandable. After all, learning the organization's vernacular is a passport of sorts, a ticket to credibility inside the organization. It can be a tough habit to break. And the longer a person spends inside the organization, the worse it can get. Sort of like a linguistic Stockholm syndrome.

Yes, there is such a thing as dumbing ideas down too much, especially when communicating peer-to-peer. Lawyers and other technical types lose patience quickly with those who, in a quest for clarity, end up stripping their writing of practically all meaning. But for general audiences, translation is usually necessary.

SPEAKING IN TONGUES

I was interviewing a manager at a manufacturing facility who started to tell me about their GMPs and their HACCP certification. I had to stop her and ask what she was talking about. She said, a little impatiently, that I needed to get up to speed on the subject matter.

Perhaps. I was thinking, though, that she needed to learn how to talk about her business to people whose first language is English.

What if I were to describe my evening at rehearsal like this?

> *Tonight at tech we were running through the blocking when the director gave me a note about my upstage cross at the top of the scene. Apparently I hit my mark late and should have cheated a little more to the audience. And I wasn't the only one—people were blowing their cues and going up all night. So now she's scheduled a cue-to-cue and a line-through every night of the run just before fight call. Somebody joked that as long as we get it right sometime before strike, we'll be in good shape.*

Understood? I didn't think so.

LET US TALK ABOUT CONTRACTIONS

This has only come up a couple of times in my career, but just in case there's any confusion, let me make this abundantly clear: it's okay to use contractions.

I was writing a speech for an executive and the head of communications (yes, communications) chuckled and assured me that of course you don't—excuse me, do not—use contractions in a speech.

Really? Who's the speaker? Socrates?

Another time I was doing voice-over work on a corporate training video and they told me that the lawyers stripped all the contractions out of the copy (which we then snuck back in).

You know who doesn't use contractions? Commander Data on *Star Trek*. Of course, he's an android. Or maybe a cyborg. Either way, we humans get to use them, whenever and wherever it sounds natural.

TAKE IT FROM DENZEL

Your duty as a plain-speaking, normal-sounding human is to communicate your ideas in simple terms that actual people will understand. If you can't do that, you need to spend more time with actual people.

As Denzel Washington put it in the movie *Philadelphia*, "Explain it to me like I'm a four-year-old."

AN ACTOR AT WORK

Conduct a More Focused Media Interview

If you want to be quoted in a news story, you need to speak in clear, simple, and concise terms. Especially to a mass media outlet, like a newspaper or television station (as opposed to a trade journal serving a specific industry). What you say needs to be easily digested by a general audience.

Take a look at some news stories and see how people are quoted. Sometimes the reporter paraphrases the source's words. Sometimes the quote is broken up into small pieces or the words are bracketed—meaning much of what the source said was unusable or so full of gibberish that it required translation.

And sometimes whole sentences

or multiple sentences are quoted. That's usually because the source kept it short, punchy, and jargon-free.

Pay special attention to what gets used in the lead paragraph or headline. That's the money quote—the catchy little sound bite that captures the essence of the story in a few words.

In preparing to speak with a reporter, think about what you'd like the headline and the lead to say. You won't always get your wish, of course, but it's a good way to boil down your message.

Explain Complex Concepts to a Layman

Always keep in mind that people outside your business or industry are not steeped in the subject matter you deal with every day. If you want them to understand, you have to put things in their terms.

Pretend you're talking to a neighbor or someone at a cocktail party. How would you explain things to them? Forget about precision and wordsmithing. Don't "lawyer" it to death—you're not on trial. Focus instead on the broader meaning of what you're trying to say.

Use analogies. Paint a mental picture. And avoid insider buzzwords, acronyms, and jargon.

A colleague helped develop a software program called Bullfighter, which is designed to search out and destroy useless corporate jargon. Some of the most offending terms she and her team identified include "best of breed," "paradigm shift," and "results driven."

One of my favorites is "action item":

> Formerly known as a 'task.' It's easier to

> talk about action than take
> it, and building 'action' into
> the name makes action even
> less probable.
> —FROM *WHY BUSINESS PEOPLE*
> *SPEAK LIKE IDIOTS,* BY BRIAN FUGERE,
> CHELSEA HARDAWAY, AND JON WARSHAWSKY

Compose a Clearer E-mail

If ever there was a time and place for plain speaking, it's e-mail. An estimated 250 billion e-mail messages are sent every day. And some days it feels like every one of those is landing in your inbox.

Make it easy on people. Keep it simple and keep it short (one screen, if possible). Use a clear, specific subject line. Tell them in the very first sentence what you want from them or what you need them to do.

There's an old journalism technique called "inverted pyramid" style. It means that the most vital information is presented up top. It's designed so editors, short of space, can simply cut from the bottom.

So in the first paragraph or two, convey the most critical facts: who, what, when, where, and why. And sometimes how. Cover the rest in descending order of importance.

Other tips: use bullet points, consider pasting attachments below the message for mobile users, and be judicious in choosing recipients.

People don't hate e-mail so much as they hate bad e-mail. Be part of the solution.

Stop Spamming People!

At its heart, speaking plainly is about respecting

your audience. One of the biggest ways to disrespect them is by wasting their time, and one of the biggest timewasters is spam.

Everybody hates getting spam, yet so many people are perpetrators themselves. I have friends who invite me to come to their shows, see their movies, and buy their stuff. Do you know how they tell me? They send e-mail after e-mail asking me to come to their shows, see their movies, and buy their stuff.

Maybe you're in charge of the office holiday party or the blood drive or getting people to turn out for an event. If you simply copy, paste, and send the same message to the same broad audience, you are no different from the guy claiming to be a Nigerian prince.

Two things you can do to make your pleas less annoying:

1 LET PEOPLE OPT OUT. Create a Facebook page or event, a LinkedIn group, a message board or an opt-in e-mail list, so that people who want the information can get it and the others won't be bothered. It's called permission marketing. There's little excuse left in this world for spamming people with information they don't care to receive.

2 BE ORIGINAL. Stop repeating the same message over and over. I wrote and produced a show that I wanted people to see. Instead of the typical "Three more chances to see my show" e-mail or message board post, I changed it up. I'd insert a picture from one of the scenes and an intriguing bit of dialogue. That is, I would give them something new, useful, or entertaining in each message. You can do the same thing:

> ■ *We just got word about a secret guest coming to the holiday party!*
>
> ■ *Bob in marketing just announced he'll provide a dollar-for-dollar match for any contribution that comes in before Friday.*
>
> ■ *Check out these new raffle prizes that have just been donated!*

Same goes for Facebook and other social media. Stop posting the same thing over and over to the same broad audience. People will block you. And if you've got a separate fan or business page, great— but don't repeat every post using your personal page. It's annoying.

SCENE 9

GETTING FROM POINT A TO POINT B

Chicago is the capital of the world for improv and sketch comedy, and at its epicenter is the famed Second City. The fifty-year-old institution has given birth to comedy legends like John Belushi, Mike Myers, and almost everyone associated with NBC's *30 Rock*.

Through its training center, Second City is also a place where thousands of regular people like me take comedy classes. I would recommend its sketch writing program to anyone who's involved or has an interest in communications of any kind. Lawyers, salespeople, and PR pros can all get something out of it—or from any kind of similar creative coursework.

I understand that for most people whose main exposure to sketch comedy is *Saturday Night Live*, discipline and focus are probably the last words that come to mind when you think of sketch.

But Second City does it really well. (If you ever get a chance to see one of their revues, do it.) And in fairness to *SNL*, they have just one week to put together their shows, while Second City spends months developing, rehearsing, testing, and fine-tuning their material.

A PREMISE-BASED STRUCTURE

Second City teaches a simple yet rigorous structure for writing a comic sketch. It starts with the foundation of a strong premise. That premise is then tested and reinforced through a series of critical turning points that escalate the action.

For example, there's a classic sketch that Steve Carell wrote (and that you can occasionally find online). Its premise: desperately lonely people will overlook any defect in a potential partner for the sake of companionship. Few things are less funny than explaining comedy, but perhaps this will be instructive.

Here's how the sketch goes:

> ■ We open on an apartment building laundry room, late at night. A woman is doing laundry and is startled by the sudden appearance of a stranger. But she gets past her fear quickly and they seem to hit it off.
>
> ■ She asks what he does for a living and he admits that he's a serial killer. Is she horrified? No, she thinks he's just teasing.
>
> ■ To prove it, he shows her a "wanted" poster with his likeness on it. Does she flee? No, she just grows increasingly fascinated. He's a killer, yes, but is he really dangerous?
>
> ■ She asks him to describe his technique and he obliges her, with a disturbing and graphic description of how he strangles his victims. Is she repulsed? Of course not! Sure, he sounds dangerous, but probably not to her, right?

■ They agree to go out on a date. She merrily skips off, pronouncing him a nice person. He turns away and grimly admits, "No, I'm really not." This may not end well!

Every point of the sketch remains true to the premise, right up to the final payoff. No matter what he says or does, she's committed to the possibility of love.

Our instructors taught us that anything that steers the story off course or undermines the premise gets cut. Even stuff that's really funny. Any humor must occur in service to the premise. Every single line, every single word must help propel the story forward to its climax and resolution.

OBJECTIVE-BASED COMMUNICATION

Just as every sketch must have a premise, every business communication requires an objective.

Your objective may be to demonstrate the organization's leadership in a certain area, explain how a change in policy will affect people's jobs, or convince a customer to buy your product.

Whatever it is, everything in the document—every word, every idea—must flow from and support that objective. Just as a joke that's funny only for the sake of being funny brings a sketch to a grinding halt, a perfectly interesting fact that's not critical to a document is just a diversion.

People are always trying to throw everything into the mix:

■ *You can't just mention a couple of departments—you have to list them all.*

■ *Why stop at three examples when you can cite seven?*

■ *What about this other really cool thing we're doing?*

And so on.

You have to constantly remind them of the objective of the piece. What's the desired outcome?

(Not) Going Out on a Limb

In the introduction to this chapter, there is a lot more I could have said about Second City and sketch comedy. I could have listed many of the other comic legends that started there, like Joan Rivers and Gilda Radner and Bill Murray.

I could have talked about some of the competing improv theaters, like IO and Annoyance, that helped many of these same people along. And I could have noted that the commonly used term "skit" is actually considered demeaning by insiders and explained why.

Possibly interesting information, all of it. But vital to the point of applying the discipline of sketch writing to business communication? No.

Picture the storyline as a tree. From start to finish you want to go in a straight line, from the roots to the top of the trunk. Time spent too far out on various branches and (God help us!) twigs is a distraction and leads to a dead end.

An Actor at Work

Keep a Document Focused and on Track

Whether you're writing web copy, a white paper, a case study or a video script, it's a good idea to start with a clearly stated objective. Get agreement on it at the outset among everyone who's going to be involved in the review and approval process.

In fact, write it at the top of the document for everyone's continued edification throughout the process. Anytime someone suggests some unnecessary addition or new direction, point back to the objective.

"Yes, it would be nice to talk about our service, but as you'll recall, the purpose of this document is to demonstrate our technology leadership. Let's save that discussion for the next one."

This is why the approval process becomes so interminable sometimes. People forget or change their minds about the document's purpose. A clear objective can help protect it from mission creep.

Deliver a Clearer Presentation

If you're using PowerPoint, structure the presentation in an outline form that's abundantly clear and easy to follow.

It's easy for an audience to get lost during a presentation. They drift off, check their messages, leave the room to take a call, or use the restroom. When they return their attention to you, they should have a good idea of where you are.

It's the old, "Tell them what you're going to say, say it, then tell them what you just said." Start with an agenda or outline slide, break the presentation up into sections, and at each section use a build slide to show where you are relative to the outline.

In this ADD age, people need guideposts.

Manage a Meeting Effectively

Every meeting should have an objective. From that objective flows a structured agenda. And someone should be in charge of enforcing that agenda.

My personal idea of hell is a rambling,

interminable meeting with no agenda and a scatter-brained moderator who indulges random tangents and distracting side issues. It's just a frustrating waste of time.

One useful technique is to appoint an "enforcer"—someone to help keep track of the time allotted for each agenda item and alert the group when things veer off course. That frees the meeting leader to focus on the substance of the discussion while someone else plays bad cop.

Keeping a meeting tight and focused—it's even better than bagels and donuts.

STAYING ON MESSAGE

There's a principle in acting called "continuity of intent." It means that in an audition or rehearsal (and especially a performance), no matter what happens—you lose your place in the script, you fumble your lines, you discover you're not wearing pants—you stay focused and in character.

So even if you have to pause and collect yourself, you're doing so as that character and in that moment. It takes a lot of composure and discipline, but mostly it's about being so completely grounded in the character and his wants and world that you're prepared for absolutely anything.

Messages function in a similar way. A message is just a boiled-down version of the point you're trying to make. It should be concise, compelling, memorable, and easily repeatable. A well-conceived set of messages grounds your communications in something solid, offering a dependable and comforting "home base" that you can return to in any situation.

The message set should also provide a framework on which you hang all your communications. Too often, messages get developed but they're not successfully integrated. They stand apart instead of being woven into communications. Or they're just tacked on as an afterthought.

That may be because they lack sufficient buy-in or they're poorly conceived. Or maybe they're too narrow in scope. Messages should be broad enough to cover a variety of circumstances. They should be about big things.

MESSAGE = STRATEGY

When I worked for the Ohio Attorney General, we had a core set of messages tied to the office's strategic goals (as all message platforms should be). Our policy priorities were fighting crime, safeguarding children, and protecting consumers, so that's where we focused our messages.

The office was big—more than a thousand employees—and had jurisdiction over at least two dozen other issue areas, from antitrust matters to taxation. All were important, but not all received the same level of attention in our communication efforts.

Some attorneys in the office wondered why we didn't make a big media splash when they had a victory. The simple answer was that it wasn't on message. So instead of a press conference with the attorney general, we might set up an interview with an Assistant AG. Or we might just issue a press release.

It didn't mean their case was any less important. It just meant we were devoting the bulk of our publicity efforts to those issues where we chose to be most visible.

Put another way, if you talk about everything, you get remembered for nothing.

MESSAGES DEFINE PRIORITIES

Some people chafe under a message framework, but I actually think it's liberating. In a world where so many issues are competing for limited attention, a solid message platform helps you prioritize your resources and channel your energy into a few core areas where you can break through and make a difference.

A message set also makes crafting communications a lot easier, as it provides a built-in structure to follow. And if an issue doesn't fit the framework, you don't talk about it—at least not proactively. (Or you find a way to shoehorn it in, but that's kind of cheating.)

WHAT MESSAGES ARE NOT

People call a lot of things messages. But messages are not long lists of bulleted items. Those are talking points. Useful, yes, but messages should be limited to three to five key points.

Messages are not paragraph after paragraph of discussion. That's a narrative. A narrative can be a useful tool, expanding on and giving context to the message framework.

Messages are not overloaded with data. Those are supporting points. "We need to reduce operating costs" is a message. "Our labor costs are twenty percent higher than those of our competitors" is a supporting point. Supporting points are important, but they're not messages.

Messages are not advertising slogans. They don't need to be fancy or cutely written. They just need to be true, they need to address the concerns of their target audience and they need to be repeated over and over and over.

ABOUT THAT DEAD HORSE

I was working with a CEO once and we brought in a high-priced "message consultant" from Washington—someone who had presidential candidates for clients. His advice was worth every penny (all 900,000 of them).

The CEO, after a full day of having key messages drilled into his head, asked, "Won't people get sick of hearing the same things over and over?" And the consultant immediately shot back, "You'll get bored long before they do."

And honestly, you should be so lucky to get this kind of complaint from your audience—it means you're actually breaking through.

Anyone who feels straitjacketed by a message set should keep in mind my favorite self-invented axiom: It's important to over-communicate because people tend to under-listen.

SEEK PROFESSIONAL HELP

There are messaging experts out there who can be of tremendous assistance. They provide an outside perspective that helps cut through the clutter. They can also do research, put the messages to the test with focus groups, and provide message training, which is vital for anyone in the spotlight.

It can be well worth it. (And it doesn't have to cost you $9,000.)

AN ACTOR AT WORK

Communicate Change

A well-constructed message set can help make the case for change with an organization's employees, shareholders, and other audiences. I've worked with companies going through challenging times and I often use a simple, four-part framework:

1 Define the reason change needs to happen (often an external threat).

2 Identify the strategy necessary to meet that threat, including what the individual can do to help.

3 Spell out the consequences (to the business and to the individual) of inaction.

4 Paint a picture of what success looks like—if we pursue this course, the payoff is [x].

Here's how the framework might come to life:

1 Threat/challenge: We're being undercut by overseas competitors with lower operating costs.

2 Strategy: To compete, we need to reduce our expenses—everyone is going to have to sacrifice.

3 Consequence: If we don't act, our market share will continue to erode and eventually we could go out of business.

4 Payoff: By taking these steps now we can stabilize the company and ensure our future security.

That's one way to do it. The key is to pick a handful of messages (no more than five), make sure they're aligned with the strategy, then just flog away until everyone's sick of hearing them.

Answer Tough Questions

It can become very easy in a crisis or in front of a group of hostile questioners (or even non-hostile ones who may simply have different priorities) to stay on message. To that I say, "Don't drop your gig!" (which is what one of my improv instructors used to call from the sidelines when we were doing scene work).

What it means is, if you step onto the stage and

make a choice—a funny accent, a limp, a fishing pole over your shoulder—you don't just randomly drop it or stop doing it.

It's the same with the message set. Never drop your gig. Always return to your messages.

If someone asks a random question, do what politicians do: answer briefly, then pivot back to the key messages:

> ■ *"Pay equity is definitely something that requires attention, but if we don't lower our operating costs it won't matter, because we'll be out of business."*
>
> ■ *"New products are important but first we have to lower our high labor costs so we can build them profitably."*
>
> ■ *"The pension issue is a problem and we're looking at it, but the truth is, if we don't take steps to strengthen our financial position, there won't be security for anyone."*

This takes discipline and poise. And practice. It's a really good idea to assemble a few members of your team and have them pepper you with questions so you can get comfortable with using the messages.

Successfully Handle a Crisis

Nothing tests message discipline like a crisis (which tends to test a lot of things—resources, energy, sanity). Conventional wisdom tells you to acknowledge early the full scope of the problem you're facing and accept responsibility.

Of course, conventional wisdom only gets you

so far, especially in unconventional situations. Some argue that getting out ahead of the story isn't the answer in all cases. One observer had this to say about the Tiger Woods scandal:

> What was Woods supposed to do? Call an immediate press conference and rattle through a list of lady friends declaring, 'Tiffany, yes; Trixy, no, Amber, don't remember ...'? And if Woods had pre-empted with a confession, would this have caused the news media, bloggers, pundits, Hooters waitresses and everyone else to collectively reward him with their silence? Not a chance.
>
> —"Not All Publicity Is Good Publicity," by Eric Dezenhall

A good point. Certain crises are so severe that the only answer is to hunker down and wait. Firestone learned that lesson back in 2000 with the Ford rollover crisis. Whatever the cause of the accidents, public perception hardened early, and no amount of communicating was going to reverse the story. Ultimately the company had to abandon the Firestone name and adopt the brand of its parent company, Bridgestone.

Messages can be powerful, but they're not magic.

SCENE 11

Using Humor

ust about every person who's ever taken an improv or sketch comedy class has encountered this reaction from people they meet: "You're a comedian? Cool. Be funny!"

Right. Be funny. Because that's all there is to it. (Which explains why so many tens of millions of Americans right now are enjoying thriving, financially lucrative careers in the comedic arts.)

Want to know the secret of comedy? Being funny is an outcome, not a goal.

Comedy = Truth

Other than professional comedians, very few people are funny when they try to be. Think of when you get together with your friends or family. How do most of those LOL moments occur? Is it when the awful brother-in-law goes,

"Hey, do you want to hear a joke?" Not bloody likely (to quote Jerry Seinfeld).

The funniest moments actually occur pretty organically, don't they? They come about through recollections of shared history and experiences: *Remember when Billy shaved the cat?* Or when someone behaves in a way that is immediately recognizable as very much in character: *That's Rob, with his computer-generated grocery list and his alphabetized sock drawer.* (Nobody I know!) Or when they act surprisingly opposite to their nature: *Who knew Grandpa could do the Lambada?*

In short, it's all about truth—connecting with some common experience or perception. Instead of trying so hard to be funny, just be true to who you are and your situation. From there, the humor will naturally emerge.

WHY HUMOR?

When done right, humor can be an excellent way to get through to people in a corporate setting.

It can help break down the defenses of a skeptical audience. And it can go a long way toward humanizing an executive. After all, if the joke's on you, you might as well be the first to tell it. By shedding light on your own foibles, you disarm your critics.

Humor is also a great way to reinforce a point and make it more memorable. Like most travelers, I usually tune out the flight attendants when they go over the emergency instructions. It's something we've all heard a thousand times, right?

But I was on an Alaska Air flight and was surprised to find they have a bit of a playful culture, not unlike Southwest Airlines. The flight attendant peppered her usual drill with some decent one-liners: *

---

* *You want to hear something kind of funny? I scribbled these notes on an airsickness bag.*

> ■ There may be fifty ways to leave your lover, but there are only eight exits off this plane.
>
> ■ If the oxygen masks come down, please first assist any child sitting next to you, or any passenger acting like a child.
>
> ■ Pardon the bumpiness as we taxi. It's not the airline's fault, it's not the pilot's fault, it's the asphalt.

I guarantee you I wasn't the only one paying attention for the first time.

Finally, humor provides at least one other important benefit: it's entertaining. There's nothing wrong with occasionally keeping an audience awake.

HOW IT CAN BE DONE

There are any number of ways to incorporate humor into your communications—conferences, training sessions, videos, speeches, awards. Here are a few tips for summoning your inner comic.

1 FIND THE TRUTH AND EXAGGERATE IT

In improv and sketch, it's called "heightening." Taking reality up a few notches until it reaches humorously absurd proportions.

For a vehicle manufacturer that wanted to illustrate to managers the unnecessary and costly complexity of its product offerings, we created a sketch where a sales rep meets with a customer and describes the available features by unraveling a one hundred-foot scroll.

From there, the conversation descends into an increasingly ridiculous series of made-up options like chinchilla-lined cup holders and such. But it was the simple image of that scroll that really drove the point home and stuck with everyone long after the meeting was over.

2 TRY PARODY OR SATIRE

Closely related to heightening is parody or satire, which is something most of us do every day—making fun of celebrities or government officials or institutions like the DMV. A tried-and-true method of using parody successfully is to play opposites.

A telecommunications client was introducing a new product development process that was designed to be simpler and more effective than the old system. We teed up the presentation with a video in which straight descriptions of the old process are countered by preposterous visuals that undercut the dialogue.

When the narrator talked about a product being fast-tracked, the video showed a turtle ambling across the screen. The company's thoughtful distribution strategy was illustrated by cargo boxes being dumped from airplanes. User training? Circus animals doing tricks. You get the picture.

You have to be careful in choosing your targets, of course. It's safer to go after subjects where there's widespread audience agreement— old practices, the competition, etc. Consultants are almost always fair game.

Of course, if the target is in the audience, he or she had better be in on the joke! (Or a reliably good sport.)

3 BE SMART ABOUT IT

One of the key principles of improv is to always play to the top of your intelligence. That means avoid going for the easy or obvious joke. (This can be a real challenge, as nine times out of ten in an improv show, when the ensemble asks the audience to suggest an occupation, someone inevitably yells, "Proctologist!")

It also means playing to the top of the audience's intelligence. It's human nature to underestimate the generic group—"Oh, *I* understand, but they'll never get it!" As a result, material gets dumbed down to the lowest common denominator. There's nothing wrong with humor that makes you think a little bit.

Another common way of underestimating the audience is to be cautious to the point of absurdity, taking the peculiar sensitivities of a couple of vocal cranks and ascribing them to the whole group. Or assuming people are unable to laugh at themselves.

I was writing a video script for a client in the direct sales business who told me that I could not use the word "ghost" because the concept was offensive to some of the devout Christians among their members.

With humor, as with life, giving people the benefit of the doubt is a smart way to go.

4 LIBERALLY ADD TOPICAL REFERENCES

Now just because dumb jokes are frowned upon doesn't mean expedient humor is necessarily a bad thing. One of the easiest—and some say cheapest—ways to get a laugh is to reference a commonly known thing or place or current event.

It's the reason people in the studio audience of a talk show spontaneously erupt in applause when their hometown is called out. "Whoa, he just said Dubuque! *I'm* from Dubuque!"

If your audience is a bunch of Northside Chicagoans and you happen to mention the Wiener's Circle, most of them will readily laugh, recalling their own late night pilgrimage to this Chicago hot dog institution where the cooks hilariously and obscenely insult the customers.

Seriously. It works every time. It almost doesn't even have to be funny—just triggering that familiar reference point can be enough to get laughs.

Sprinkle your presentations or copy with a few well-chosen references to the headline of the day or the most despised entrée in the company cafeteria or the CEO's fondness for breeding labradoodles, and you are, as they say, money, my friend (*Swingers* reference).

5 DO A CALLBACK

This is another cheap one. A callback is simply a reference to an earlier joke—ideally one that got a good laugh the first time. (Though Johnny

Carson used to get tons of mileage in his monologues by doing repeated callbacks to a joke that bombed, I don't recommend that approach for mere mortals. Move on.)

Like the topical reference, the callback creates a shared experience among the audience members. When they get it, they feel smart and part of the in-crowd.

The Office does callbacks all the time, to the delight of the show's rabid fans. When Michael Scott goes undercover to engage in a little corporate espionage, he identifies himself as Michael Scarn, who loyal viewers will recall was the central character in his spy movie screenplay, *Threat Level: Midnight.* The ultimate payoff came a full five seasons after the original reference with the unveiling of the final film.

This works well at meetings and conferences, where you can reference events or remarks that occurred earlier. "Ed talked this morning about the need to rein in costs and I can't help but think he was talking about the $29,000 Berber carpet in my office."

The farther removed the callback is, the more effective it can be. So putting a twist on something from a day or two before is better than riffing on your own material just minutes later. You can go back even farther, as long as the thing you're referencing is sufficiently memorable.

Say you're at your company's annual meeting, and the big controversy that everyone remembers from last year is that they ran out of desserts at lunchtime. (And it's always those little annoying things that are most remembered.) You might say, "After this session, we go into lunch... and don't worry, we have been assured by a team of auditors from the international accounting firm of PriceWaterhouseCoopers that there are exactly 1.5 desserts on hand for each person here."

6 BE SPECIFIC

Instinct would tell you that the more general and universal you are, the more likely you will appeal to the widest audience. Not true, actually. The more specific you are, the more real you are. And truthful. And thus funny. Even if people don't exactly get the reference, there's something about specificity that's inherently funny.

Take *Seinfeld.* What's funnier than being offered a beverage? Being offered a Snapple. What's funnier than an heiress? An O Henry candy bar heiress. What's funnier than Florida? Del Boca Vista.

Think about the equivalent specifics in your organization. Don't just say, "Man, I hate filling out expense reports!" Talk about the weird requirement that everyone hates—"Receipts must be glue-sticked, not scotch-taped." Don't complain about the food in the cafeteria— expound on the dreaded "Tuesday Pork Surprise."

This is the most overused "go-to" for desperate improvisers. When stuck for something to say or do, they offer someone a mimed Fresca or muse over their imaginary Trio Salad from Corner Bakery. Gets them every time.

God, as they say, is in the details. But don't let that intimidate you or anything.

7 BEWARE OF THE HUMOR-IMPAIRED

I generally feel that everyone has a sense of humor. If they can't tell a joke, they can at least appreciate one—just like a person who can't carry a tune can enjoy listening to music.

But I've worked with people who have put that belief to the test. People who aren't very funny (or smart) should not edit other people's humor. They can suggest, they can question, they can argue, but they should in no way be able to re-word or revise the joke.

The humor-impaired will gut your set-ups, mess with your rules-of-three and bury your punch lines. The lesson? If you don't get the joke, you don't get to fix the joke.

SERIOUS BUSINESS

Obviously, humor is out of the question for some topics, like explaining your company's response to an indictment or a product recall or an environmental disaster. But otherwise I think much of what we communicate, particularly to employees, and especially anything they're going to have to sit through for hours, can benefit from the judicious (and well-executed) use of humor.

On the other hand (and speaking of judicious), I used to go observe oral arguments in the U.S. Supreme Court as part of my job with the National Association of Attorneys General. I distinctly recall a number of very funny moments where the justices joked with counsel or each other, prompting rounds of laughter in the courtroom. So even the highest echelon of our most-respected branch of government isn't too stodgy for a little humor.

In my opinion, just about the worst character flaw for an individual or an organization is to take yourself—as distinguished from the work you do—too seriously.

AN ACTOR AT WORK

Enliven a Conference

Multi-day conferences can be deadly without something fun to break up the action. I've worked on conferences where we set everything within the format of a talk show or newscast or featured recurring characters from pop culture. (A faux Forrest Gump is forever embedded in my memory. How many aspects of business would you guess are like a box of chocolates?)

This framing device is a great way to keep things moving, reinforce messages, and provide comic relief. To be done well, it usually requires professional hosts, actors, writers, and elaborate staging and sets. It's a big production, but a wise investment if you want to keep people engaged in your content instead of hovering over the snack tables.

On a smaller scale, a financial services client had an annual meeting where the division head and his direct reports would present their end-of-year results in the form of a game. One year it was extreme sports, another was high stakes poker. (Jai alai was even on the drawing board at some point.)

All it required was some professional scripting, a few costumes and equipment, and the willingness of the executives to put themselves out there with ridiculous puns like "I'm all in," "I've got an ace up my sleeve," and "Let's go to the flop."

You can also break the monotony with top ten lists, song parodies, and comic sketches. If you're willing to spend lots of money you can even get someone like David Letterman or Conan O'Brien to write and record a custom bit for you.

Make Training Fun

Learning should be fun. A client's IT department was forever challenged with getting people to use new technology and software. In another testament to the creativity that resides in the most unexpected places, those IT geeks decided, completely on their own, to create a game show-formatted trivia contest.

Different floors of the office competed in front of a panel of judges and a cheering audience. Teams were quizzed on their technical expertise and knowledge of various software programs and winners received trophies, gift cards, and cash.

Another client had a three-day training course for its global sales force and wanted to keep the sessions lively and interesting. I played a recurring character who would pop in via video at various points to reinforce messages, tee up content, and just mix things up a bit.

Capture It on Tape

Your own employees may represent a vast untapped source of quality humor. I've had great success running do-it-yourself employee video contests.

You can make it as low or high budget as you want. Create whatever incentives you can afford—an extra day off, a pizza party, a trip to Vegas. Provide equipment or let people use their own cameras or smartphones. You can recruit students from a local college film department for low-cost videography and editing.

The videos can be used for internal meetings and office parties, shown at award ceremonies, posted on your Intranet site, or externally on your website or YouTube. Ideally they should have some strategic purpose, of course—illuminating an issue, highlighting a policy, attracting customers, etc.

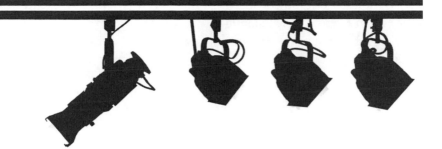

GRAMMAR PEEVES

read a lot of online commentary about the TV shows I follow, and sometimes the purists who point out tiny plot holes and inconsistencies can get a little annoying.

"There's no way Coach Taylor should have called a pass play in that situation—didn't any of the writers play football?" (Answer: of course they didn't!) Or *"I worked on Madison Avenue in 1964 and I can tell you for certain nobody had a chrome and glass coffee table in their office!"*

As the Comic Book Guy from *The Simpsons* would say, "Worst episode ever!"

That's me when it comes to grammar.* Yup, I'm that guy.

But I think we all have a bit of the grammar cop in us. We love to point out other people's violations. We can't resist

---

Disclaimer: I am prepared for the eventuality that readers may find errors aplenty in this book, if not on this very page. I don't claim to be perfect. Except when it comes to my own personal peeves.

the articles that pop up constantly online—Ten Grammar Mistakes You Don't Even Know You're Making!

So grab some popcorn and follow along as I present a few of my pet peeves.

A CAVEAT

Keep in mind that proper grammar and usage is an unpopular cause and a no-win battle in the face of an evolving language and a mostly indifferent public.

Knowing what's correct will not make you appear smarter. Nor will it necessarily give you a leg up in the organization or improve your value in the marketplace.

And it definitely won't make you more popular. In fact, pointing these things out will earn you, at best, quizzical looks and, at worst, a reputation for snobbery. The sole reward you will get from this information is the satisfaction of knowing you're right. It's up to you how smug this satisfaction will make you feel.

Just keep in mind that when you do this, in the eyes of most people, you're basically the Comic Book Guy. So it's probably best to just keep it to yourself.

THESE EIGHT WORDS
ARE NOT LIKE THE OTHERS

There/their, it's/its, lose/loose—child's play. Here's an advanced course on confusing word pairs.

- Lend/Loan. *Lend* is a verb, *loan* is a noun. You never loan anyone something. You lend it to them. Just as you don't apply for a lend.
- Tack/tact. *Tack* is a nautical term meaning to adjust course on a sailboat. So you take a different tack, not tact (which I suppose people believe is a shortened form of *tactic*).

- Jibe/jive. There must be something about the sea that causes confusion. So while your figures may not *jibe* with hers, *jive* is a whole other thing entirely. As in "Don't give me that jive," "Oh, stewardess, I speak jive," and "Back off, you jive turkey." (You could probably hear all these different uses in just one episode of *Good Times*.)

- Hone/Home. You hone an idea, while you home in on a solution. *Hone* means to sharpen.

- Comprise/compose. Hardly anyone gets this right. "The book is comprised of twenty-five chapters" is wrong. Say "composed of." (Or better yet, just say the book *has* twenty-five chapters.) Here is a proper use of *comprise*: "The neighborhood comprises five hundred houses." Weird, huh? Just take my advice and don't bother using comprise at all. Chances are you'll do it incorrectly.

- Regards/Regarding. *Regards* are what you offer people in good cheer or fondness ("Give my regards to...") Regards is NOT a synonym for "regarding." Simply say, "In regard to." No *s*. Ever.

- Everyday/every day. Believe it or not, these are two different concepts. *Everyday* means ordinary or commonly occurring while *every day* means each and every single day. Sly Stone assures us that in spite of his fame and lifestyle, he is simply "everyday people." Elvis Costello, unfortunately, gets it wrong when he sings, "Everyday I write the book." Clearly he means every day. It's sad to think of how many record sales this cost him.

- Yeah/yea. When said out loud, *yeah* does not rhyme with hay. *Yeah* is slacker for yes. If you want to say, in effect, "yippie," you spell it y-e-a. For ultimate clarity, do what I do. Spell it the informal (yet still acceptable) way: yay.

THREE THINGS ABOUT NUMBERS

My annoyance at these errors cannot be quantified.

■ It's "ten items or *fewer*," not less. There's not a grocery store in America that has gotten this right. *Fewer* is generally for things you can count—people, books, cats. *Less* is for more vague comparisons of degree. He is *less* handsome, *less* charming, *less* interesting (especially when he talks about grammar).

■ Understand the important difference between a percentage and percentage points. A candidate who wins the popular vote fifty-seven to forty-two percent has not won by fifteen percent. Those are percentage points. In terms of true percentage, he actually won by almost thirty-six percent.

■ A major weakness of the overly left-brained is to cite dates and statistics with wholly unnecessary precision. "Congress passed the reform legislation on September 20, 2007." Who cares? Unless you're making a point about that specific date, just call it "the 2007 legislation." Same with statistics. Instead of "sixty-eight percent," say "more than two-thirds." Instead of "forty-seven percent," use "nearly half." And watch for the misuse of approximately. On what planet is "approximately 62.3 percent" at all approximate?

THREE PERENNIAL PUNCTUATION PROBLEMS

Here's how to handle some of those troublesome non-letter squiggly things.

■ "Commas and periods always go inside quotation marks," I say to you.

■ Periods belong outside parentheses when the parenthetical is part of a larger sentence (if you get what I mean). (Though when the parenthetical stands alone as its own sentence, the opposite is true.)

■ There is no apostrophe in the plural forms of numerals and initialisms.* So it's CEOs, DVDs and 1990s. To the dismay of purists worldwide, the *New York Times* regularly violates this rule and manages nevertheless to win the occasional Pulitzer.

I'LL TAKE POTPOURRI FOR 500, ALEX

A few miscellaneous matters of usage and grammar to ponder.

■ People who don't know the proper use of *I* versus *me* (as in "she and I," "you and me," etc.) inevitably default to *I* in all situations, thinking, I suppose, that it just sounds more intelligent. (Reality show contestants are a group that seems to suffer especially from this malady—"What happened in the hot tub is between Jake and I.") Here's a simple tip. Take the other person out of the sentence and the answer becomes obvious. "The gift is from ~~Jessica and~~ me," "~~You and~~ I need to have a talk." And in case you do get chosen for *The Bachelor*, it is never, ever, "Between you and I." Ever.

■ Here's one I see in the first line of almost every pitch letter or fundraising appeal I read. When you say, "As a technology expert, I thought you'd be

---

Many people refer to any initialism, or abbreviation using the first letter of each word being abbreviated, as an acronym. But, strictly speaking, acronyms are only abbreviations that spell out a pronounceable word on their own, like NATO (North Atlantic Treaty Organization) and radar (Radio Detection and Ranging). Standards seem to have loosened so that almost any abbreviation made up of letters, like FBI and CIA, is labeled an acronym, but you and I know better, don't we?

interested in our latest offering," you're actually saying that *you* are the technology expert, not the person you're writing to and trying to butter up. Instead, say, "As a technology expert, you might be interested..."

■ Stop saying, "I'd like to thank" or "I want to congratulate." If you really want to do these things, just do them and stop talking about doing it. Try "I'm thankful to," "Thanks to," "I'm grateful to," "I congratulate."

■ When you're writing to someone who's got higher status than you or if you're asking something of them, don't say, "Please don't hesitate to call." Your CEO or your customer doesn't need your permission or assurance that it's okay to call you. To offer it is presumptuous. Just say, "Please call me." (Better yet: you call them.)

■ Unless you're thirteen, *anyways* is never correct under any circumstance.

Four Mistakes That Are Not Mistakes

Stop listening to your sixth-grade English teacher.

■ Feel free to split your infinitives—it's perfectly acceptable. Otherwise you end up with tortured prose like this example I came across online: "Permit me respectfully to disagree."

■ There is nothing at all wrong with sentence fragments. Especially in more informal writing and marketing copy. It adds variety.

■ Beginning a sentence with a conjunction helps break up long sentences. And a thought that stands alone gets extra emphasis. But don't do it all the time. Or it will become tiresome.

■ Winston Churchill is quoted (perhaps erroneously) saying this about the old-fashioned prohibition against ending sentences with a preposition: "This is a rule up with which I will not put."

WHAT'S THE POINT?

Does grammar matter anymore? Some argue that in this age of quick texts and posts and tweets, it's the intention that counts, not the presentation.

In an earlier chapter, I discussed a memo from David Mamet. When I first read it, I was appalled at his terrible grammar and sloppy punctuation. And yet, not a single Broadway theater has rejected his work based on that. There is no justice in this world.

If you've got Mamet-level talent in your field, you can probably get away with a lot of things. For the rest of us, it's better to be safe than sorry. You never know when you'll run into a purist.

And even non-purists will wonder what else you might be careless about. So mind your (apostrophe-free) *P*s and *Q*s.

AN ACTOR AT WORK

Beware the Online Grammar Virus

The online world is about immediacy and impact. Give them the gist and never mind the mechanics, right?

Maybe so. But be careful. These habits can become hard to break and they can easily bleed over into your more formal communications.

I used to read a blogger who had

pretty interesting stories to tell but had absolutely atrocious grammar. One of her many tics was using commas where dashes, semi-colons, and even periods should go.

I think it was intentional—a way to make her copy flow quickly and briskly. But I had to stop following her blog, not only because it was annoying, but because I found I was starting to get confused about punctuation myself.

Sloppy writing can be contagious.

Put Your Best Foot Forward

For resumes, cover letters, business proposals, websites, and other formal communications, proper grammar, spelling, and punctuation are still important.

Even if you think that stuff doesn't or shouldn't matter, there are still many people who do. And since those people tend to be older, they're often in decision-making positions. They view glaring errors as an indication of carelessness, inattention to detail, laziness—you name it.

And if you're a writer or communications professional, you should know that your cover letter, resume, and thank you note are actually writing tests. When I worked in the PR firm, we'd get resumes all the time with typos and other errors. We would rarely call those candidates in for an interview.

Don't Be That Guy

This one's simple. Don't correct other people's grammar in public. Nothing good can come from that.

ACT IV IV IV IV I

GET ME REWRITES!

"This applies to many film jobs, not just editing: half the job is doing the job, and the other half is finding ways to get along with people and tuning yourself in to the delicacy of the situation."

—Walter Murch, film editor

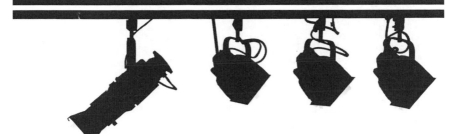

SCENE 12

SLASH AND BURN

n the film *The Fugitive*, there's a memorable scene in which the federal marshal, played by Tommy Lee Jones, corners Harrison Ford's Dr. Richard Kimble down in the bowels of a giant hydroelectric dam. Kimble yells, "I didn't kill my wife!" and the marshal replies simply, "I don't care!"

That's it. That's the essence of the film right there in those two lines: a man on the run out to prove his innocence versus the lawman sworn to bring him to justice.

But apparently the original script included a bunch of dialogue that was ultimately cut on set. I don't know what those lines were, but let's imagine it was another (very bad) screenwriter and it went like this:

KIMBLE: I didn't kill my wife!

MARSHAL: I don't care!

KIMBLE: What do you mean you don't care?

MARSHAL: It's not my responsibility. You see, the way the Justice Department is structured—

KIMBLE: So it doesn't matter to you whether I'm guilty or innocent?

MARSHAL: Technically, no. My job isn't to determine guilt or innocence, but to track down federal fugitives.

KIMBLE: But you could be sending an innocent man to prison.

MARSHAL: I have to leave that to others to sort out. My only duty is to bring you in.

KIMBLE: It doesn't bother you that you could be contributing to a grave miscarriage of justice?

MARSHAL: I find if I let those kinds of considerations enter into my mind it distracts me from my job, which is to—

KIMBLE: I know, I know, I get it!

See? Even Kimble's bored with all this unnecessary exposition. And he's kind of a captive audience!

WORDS, WORDS, WORDS

This is something I battle with every day. I hate cutting my stuff.

I long for the age when advertisers crammed hundreds of words on a magazine page, telling great epic stories about the heartbreak of psoriasis.

Cutting is hard. Some of us get emotionally attached to our own words.

For others, it's less a matter of attachment than detachment. Detachment from reality. No matter how many times you tell them about space limitations and maximum word counts they seem to think that by cutting ten words they can add two hundred.

Like it or not, this is the direction the world continues to move in—less and less space for text. So what to do about it?

Eliminate the "How"

Lawyers, consultants, and technology types are often dismayed to learn that nobody really cares about their "process." People are much more interested in results. It's the old line about the legislative process: nobody wants to see how the sausage is made.

Or as a colleague put it during a particularly arduous editing project: "It's like reading about the history of dentistry. The only person interested in that is the dentist, not the patient."

So unless you're specifically writing a "how-to" manual, the first place to cut is the long description of your proprietary five-point process. Focus instead on what truly matters to your audience: how your product or service will improve their lives or how the information or insights you're delivering will benefit them.

Learn to Love Your Graphic Designers

Or at least understand them. They're trying to ensure that your writing actually gets read. Dumping a bunch of words in their lap and expecting them to make it all "look nice" is a recipe for...well, if not disaster, at least a really ugly document that nobody reads.

In the ideal world, content development and graphic design go hand-in-hand, each complementing and informing the other. Usually, though, the designer gets stuck at the end of the process trying to turn the proverbial sow's ear into a silk purse.

Occasionally it works the other way around. The design is done first, irrespective of the actual copy. I was actually told once to add words when my copy didn't fit the prescribed template.

Either way, be open to the designer's ideas—especially when they say, "We need more white space." It's that pleasant empty area that makes your words less intimidating to read.

I've worked for a long time with a creative director who has a great instinct both for design and copy. He has always pushed me to cut. At first it was difficult, but it's actually been a big help. Because there is almost always *something* that can go.

But That's My Baby!

In the deleted scenes commentary to *The Sixth Sense*, director M. Night Shyamalan relates a lesson he learned in film school: always be prepared to cut your favorite scene. It's tough to do, but if it doesn't serve the larger story, it has to go.

All of us at some point love things and people that are no good for us. It's the same with words and ideas. Hold them up to greater scrutiny. Ask yourself why you love them so much.

It may be that they're really, really good. Or it could be you're so enamored of them that you've lost your ability to be objective.

Won't Someone Think of the Readers!?

But this paragraph is so awesome! It would be tragic for readers not to see it!

Here's a little something I learned from doing theater. At some point during a show's run (maybe even at several points), somebody's going to drop a line or two of dialogue. Actors will beat themselves up over it—especially if it's a really good or really funny line. *O, poor audience! I've deprived them of this beautiful moment!*

But when we do that, we're not really thinking about it from the audience's perspective. We miss the line because we knew and loved the line. But the audience is none the wiser and no worse off. (Unless the line conveyed a major plot point, of course.) So that's the way to look at it: it's impossible for them to miss something they never knew existed in the first place.

MAKING CHOICES

Learning to edit yourself—to be objective about your own work—is hard. But writing (like art and, for that matter, life) is about choices. Make them.

For the record, I cut 12.7 percent of the words from the first draft of this chapter.

AN ACTOR AT WORK

Cut Down Your Videos

Keep your videos short, short, short. Especially if you're posting them online. YouTube is absolutely killing the already limited human attention span. So even if you're convinced you've got the next viral "Star Wars Kid" or "Keyboard Cat" on your hands, limit your online videos to one or two minutes at most.

One effective way to do this is to structure a longer video so it can be broken up into small sections for easier consumption. Separate the videos by topic or by interview subject and let people click on the thumbnails that interest them.

The same goes for videos shown in front of a group. A client once said that it was okay for their video to be ten minutes long since they were showing it to employees in a meeting—a "captive audience," he said.

I've got news for you: just because employees don't physically walk out, that doesn't mean they're not mentally checked out. When you create videos that are going to be shown live, organize them into short sections and intersperse discussion and interaction between them.

Trim Your Writing

Challenge yourself to make cuts in everything you write. Assume that it can always be shorter, and that shorter is always better.

Set a goal of cutting ten percent of your words. Or twenty percent, if you're feeling really ambitious. Try to limit paragraphs to two sentences, memos to one page, e-mails and web copy to a single screen.

Here's a really radical approach. I went to a panel discussion of sketch comedy directors where one of them recommended that when we finish writing a sketch and are really happy with it, we should tear it up and start over.

This sounds suspiciously like one of those pieces of advice that the advice giver himself never actually follows. I haven't tried it—at least not deliberately. But I have, like everyone, lost countless documents and e-mails when the computer crashes or I do something careless or stupid.

And when I go back to recreate them, I've often found the second version really is better. It's sharper and more concise. I think it's because words are harder to part with when they're right there in front of us. And cutting is messy—it leaves a hole that needs to be patched up.

Starting from a clean slate is risky, but if you've

got the time, go for it. (Though I'd keep the old draft around just in case.)

Shorten Your Speeches

Speeches are designed to be delivered aloud. So the sooner in the drafting process that you start reading it out loud, the better.

This will not only help you catch tongue twisters and awkward turns of phrase, it can help you pare the text down, too.

We're much more forgiving when we read silently to ourselves. We skip things, we tune out, we rush. But when you force yourself to read it out loud, word for word, at a normal speaking pace, you begin to spot the places where it drags.

Pay special attention to these parts. If they bore you, chances are very good they'll bore your audience. Partly because the content probably is boring, but also because if you're not inspired, you won't be putting the necessary energy behind it to keep people engaged.

Be sure to time it. Try to come in under your allotted time. Nobody has ever walked out of a meeting thinking, "Man, I wish that speech had been longer!"

And if there's going to be Q&A, allow at least a third of your time for it. If no Q&A is scheduled, see if you can change that.

SCENE 13

EDIT UNTO OTHERS

he worst director I ever worked with did little more than bark out orders and instructions. Start upstage. Say your first line. Turn away. Cross to stage left. Say your next line.

To put it mildly, that approach didn't inspire my best performance.

The best director I ever worked with asked a lot of questions and engaged the actors in an ongoing conversation. *Why do you think your character reacts that way? What do you suppose that line means? That's an interesting choice—what if we tried this?*

It was a collaborative approach. It forced us to fully participate and gave us a sense of ownership. In the end, we learned more and developed faster.

In business, very few people get the kind of direction they need in order to become better writers. There's a serious shortage of good editing.

Why We Don't Edit

Some people don't edit very well, and some don't edit at all.

People often say they don't have enough time to edit. But if you believe that we make the time for the things we consider a priority, you should be able to carve out enough of it for something so important—even in the most frenetic office environment.

People also don't edit because it involves confrontation and conflict. It's the same reason we don't like to do performance reviews. Finding constructive ways to offer criticism and put people on a path to improvement is hard work.

And few people are trained for it. In many organizations, especially smaller workplaces, training opportunities of any kind—let alone for writing and editing—are usually of the informal, on-the-job variety.

How to Be a Better Editor

Just because you're a good writer doesn't mean you're a good editor. *
The two disciplines are very different. Editing requires objectivity, a critical eye, and people skills, among other things.

Aside from simply making and taking the time to do it, here are some things you can do to be a better editor.

1 Discuss it face-to-face. First and foremost, instead of just marking up a document and handing or sending it back, take the time to sit down with people to provide context and explanation and give them an opportunity to respond. It should be a two-way conversation. Otherwise, by not pointing out patterns and problem areas, you're going to be seeing the same issues over and over again.

---

*Which brings to mind the T.S. Eliot quote, "I suppose some editors are failed writers; but so are most writers."

2 EDIT, DON'T REWRITE. We get so caught up in our own vision of the way things should be, we end up being rewriters instead of editors. Instead of just striking out copy and scribbling additions in the margins, make suggestions and ask questions (or, if using the "track changes" function in Microsoft Word, make liberal use of the "comments" feature):

> ■ *We could use a stronger lead—what's the most important point to emphasize?*
>
> ■ *This is phrased awkwardly. How can we put it better?*
>
> ■ *Not sure this example supports the argument we're making. Find a better connection.*

3 DON'T EDIT FOR THE SAKE OF EDITING. Though just about any document can stand improvement and benefit from other perspectives, there's often a tendency to make changes simply for the sake of appearing to make a contribution. This is one of the perils of a track changes document that gets passed along from person to person. If we're not adequately represented with our own color-coded markups, people might think we're slacking.

4 EDIT EARLY. The time to edit a document is when it's in Word form, not when it's designed and laid out and about to go to print. That's the time for proofing. Incorporating major changes is more difficult, more costly and more likely to produce errors. I see this problem all the time. I think it's partly a matter of procrastination and partly a failure to think abstractly—"Oh, I didn't know it was going to look like *that!*" So even if you're going to edit often, make it a point to edit early.

5 BE RESPONSIVE AND REALISTIC. Don't sit on a document for two weeks and then demand your changes be made in twenty-four hours. Especially if you're late in giving feedback. Also annoying are the people who drag their feet on reviewing a document then return it with comments right before the holidays. It's fine to clear your desk but don't expect people to interrupt their vacation because you waited until the last minute.

6 ASSUME KNOWLEDGE. If some piece of information surprises you or conflicts with what you know, don't assume it's wrong. It's entirely possible the writer, by immersing herself in the subject matter, has picked up something you don't know. Ask where she got the information and if she's sure of the facts.

7 ASSUME INNOCENCE. If something doesn't meet your expectations, don't assume it's because the writer is lazy or ill-informed. All too often our first reaction is a negative one, especially when we're under a lot of stress. Don't speculate about motivation; talk about results. This is just good people management.

8 DO UNTO OTHERS. We've all had the experience where a boss or a client—especially one a couple of steps removed from the process—orders up a litany of changes to a document that don't make any sense. They're so far out of the loop that they're making suggestions based on incorrect data or ancient information or already-discarded ideas. Don't be that guy. Break the chain.

GOOD EDITOR, GOOD EDITEE

Now that you've learned how to be a good editor, return the favor to those who edit you.

Nobody wants to be labeled as "difficult," the Sean Young * of the business world. But that's just what happens to people who fight tooth and nail over every little change to a document they've written.

Keep in mind that this is business, not art, and you're not Shakespeare. Choose your battles, be ready to compromise, and learn to let it go.

As an actor, I get told "no" something like ten or fifteen times for every "yes." That's the nature of the audition process. It's excellent preparation for business and for life, where you can't always get what you want.

If you're working in anything bigger than a sole proprietorship, you'd better get used to the idea that other people—your boss, your colleagues, your board, your lawyers—are going to mess with your beautiful prose.

Disputing the small stuff is a tremendous waste of time and energy. Not to mention your credibility, if you get tagged as overly defensive or unable to be objective about your own work.

The result may be a document that's less than ideal. But pragmatism is more important than purity, and style must sometimes take a back seat to substance.

And who knows? Their input might actually improve the work. So suppress your initial defensive instinct and take the time to really consider the feedback you receive.

Do the Right Thing

No amount of attention from an editor can make a bad writer good. But a lot of decent writers—people who have the basic skills— can learn to be better writers with a little constructive guidance.

Aside from all the knowledge and skill required, much of being a good editor comes down to being a good manager: understanding

---

*If you don't know who Sean Young is, there's a simple reason for that: she was difficult. But be sure to rent No Way Out for a glimpse of her early potential.

people as individuals, figuring out what motivates and inspires them, learning their style and adjusting ours accordingly for best results.

It's also about being a good human being. Treating people decently and fairly. Being honest yet tactful. Engaging them instead of dictating to them.

We hear the complaint all the time that people—often "the kids these days"—don't know how to write. We can blame bad parenting or inadequate schooling or the Internet. But there's at least one thing that's within our power to do: help them get better.

AN ACTOR AT WORK

Edit Documents with Care

Another reason it's important to edit instead of rewrite is that the author generally knows the document better than anyone else.

So you may add a point without realizing it's already stated elsewhere. Or you may cut something without understanding its impact on the rest of the document.

When you hack a paragraph or a sentence out of a well-written document, it's like cutting a section out of a bridge. Suddenly you've got two ideas left dangling on either end. They need to be connected by a proper transition.

So make suggestions, and leave the execution to the writer. And if you do rewrite, it's yours now—you own it. Don't make a mess of the document over two or three drafts and hand it back to the original author for "cleanup."

Be Reasonable with Videos

Unless they're done on the cheap or guerrilla-style, videos are exceptionally complicated productions. Ordering up changes isn't like editing a document.

So be realistic in the edits you demand. Unless you're prepared to invest in a re-shoot, which is really expensive, understand that you're limited to the footage that's "in the can."

Which is why it's really important to pay attention in the planning phase to make sure you get what you expect. But keep in mind that even the best Hollywood directors don't always get what they want. A thousand contingencies, from the weather to someone's bad day, can interfere and force compromises.

Coach a Better Performance

Providing feedback on someone's speaking skills, whether a speech by your boss or a sales pitch by a direct report, can be tricky. Even more than their writing, people are sensitive about how they appear and are perceived by others.

So it's important to be constructive and tactful. Point out their strong points before correcting their problems. And don't overwhelm them—boil the feedback down into categories, or focus on the three most important things.

Try to present third-party observations to validate what you're saying. If there are formal audience evaluations of a speech, use those. Otherwise, seek out anecdotal feedback that you can share.

If feasible, record the performance on video so they can see for themselves. There's nothing more enlightening than truly seeing yourself as others see you.

For hard cases, you can always enlist allies by hiring a professional performance coach and signing them up for training.

If You Dish It Out, Learn to Take It

Accept feedback with grace and ease. Remember Michael Corleone's words in *The Godfather*: "It's not personal, it's business."

Approach the process as a negotiation. Choose your battles and focus on those things you feel most strongly about. Let the others go. Compromising is not only a good thing for the document and the process, it has the added benefit of making you appear reasonable.

And as with any negotiation, learn to read the other person's personality and mood. Listen to their concerns and push back if necessary. But respect their limits and their tolerance for disagreement.

ACT V

ACTION!

"*They're moving pictures, let's make 'em move!*"
—Howard Hawks, film director

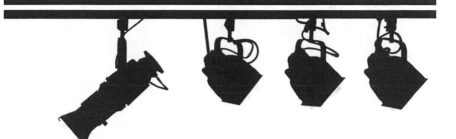

SCENE 14

OVERCOMING BARRIERS TO COMMUNICATION

ne of the first and most important lessons taught in improv is to always come from a "place of yes." That is, when something is introduced in a scene, you agree with it. So if your scene partner says, "Man, it's hot out here!" you can respond in one of two ways:

- Right: *"Yeah, I'm sweating like a Pennsylvania steelworker in July!"*
- Wrong: *"Really? I find the temperature quite agreeable."*

Beginning improv classes are filled with people denying the action that's established:

- *"What do you mean, it's raining? We're inside!"*

■ *"Why are you speaking in that fake British accent?"*
■ *"No, I'm not actually dead, I'm just pretending to be dead."* *

I know, because I've committed all these sins and more.

The reason you're taught to be positive is that denying what's going on simply stops the scene dead in its tracks. By committing to the concept of "yes, and" (agreeing and adding a little something more), you keep the scene moving forward.

Don't Fear the Speaker

In the corporate world, we run into these scene stoppers every day. They throw up petty roadblocks to communication. They deliberately drag their feet. They order endless edits to documents.

These are people who come from a place of no. It's like the title on their business card reads, "Devil's Advocate in Chief." Maybe it makes them feel smarter. Or perhaps they find comfort in the status quo.

I believe resistance to communication is mainly based on fear. Fear of change. Fear of saying the wrong thing. Fear of seeming ignorant and uninformed. Fear of looking stupid in front of a bunch of people.

This fear manifests itself in a variety of excuses that people and organizations use to avoid communicating. Let's shoot holes through them, shall we?

We Don't Have Time

Lack of time, of course, is the mother of all excuses, and certainly not exclusive to communications. I have almost zero tolerance for people who say they don't have time to do something. We make time for the things that are important. If someone isn't making the time to

---

* *For a frighteningly realistic depiction of bad improv, see the "E-mail Surveillance" episode of* The Office *in which Michael Scott shoots and kills every single one of his scene partners. Talk about coming from a place of no!*

communicate, they don't consider it a priority.

Or as Lao Tzu, the ancient father of Taoism (and an eminently quotable guy), put it, "Time is a created thing. To say 'I don't have time,' is like saying, 'I don't want to.'"

Anyone who complains about not having enough time in a day had better not spend a moment on Facebook or in front of the TV.

WE DON'T HAVE ALL THE INFORMATION

Really? When does anyone ever have the luxury of having all the necessary facts at hand? I rarely do. Even in an age where the information spigot is always turned on and always gushing data.

If you sit around waiting for the perfect storm of knowledge and information, be prepared for an awfully long wait. Perfect storms are called that because they tend to be the exceptions to the rule.

Yes, preparation is important, but being one hundred percent prepared for anything is increasingly out of reach. The best you can do is tell people what you know when you know it and promise to get them the rest of the information as soon as you get it.

Silence is not a good alternative. Like nature, gossip abhors a vacuum.

THEY'LL ASK A QUESTION
WE CAN'T ANSWER

So what? What is with this fear people have of being labeled stupid or uninformed or out of the loop just because they can't answer a question?

Let me share three little words you can use to answer any question in the universe. But you have to be secure enough to say them. The words are, "I don't know."

Back at the PR firm I had a boss—a pretty senior-level guy, number two in the office—who demonstrated a startling capacity to admit when he didn't have an answer for something. At first I was dumbfounded, but I soon grew to respect it. What a powerful demonstration of self-confidence! He didn't worry about what anybody thought.

And what a relief when compared with all the people who BS their way through an answer, demonstrating that they, too, don't know—only with twenty times the words.

Of course, "I don't know" should be followed quickly by, "But I'll find out and get back to you."

THE LAWYERS WON'T LET US

I love lawyers. Some of my best friends—and clients—are lawyers. But bad lawyers can be a huge obstacle to getting things done. And even good lawyers can be difficult if you don't know how to deal with them effectively.

Here's a little secret for you: a lawyer's words are an *opinion*. It may be a well-informed opinion. Or not. Either way, it's that one lawyer's view based on his or her interpretation of the law. And his or her personal tolerance for risk. Other lawyers may have other perspectives.

Some lawyers are more conservative than others. Some have been burned badly by careless and loose-lipped people. Some just don't understand the basic principles of PR and communications. Some are too busy to deal with it. Some are totally correct. But you'll never find out unless you push them a little.

THEY'VE ALREADY BEEN TOLD

Have they really? How and by whom? And if they have been told, do they understand? Don't assume.

A message requires lots of impressions before it sticks. It has to come through multiple channels and multiple sources. One e-mail or web posting or newsletter article won't cut it.

There's an old, and possibly sexist, story about a man and wife who have been married for years. She complains, "You never tell me you love me." He replies, "I told you I loved you the day we got married. If the situation ever changes, I'll let you know."

It's important not to be that guy. Communicate like it's your job. (Because for most of us, it is.)

I'VE GOT WRITER'S BLOCK

I hate to break it to you, but there is no such thing as writer's block.

I know, I know, you've seen the movies with the tortured artist holed up in his mountain cabin staring helplessly out the window, an intimidating pile of blank white paper in front of him.

Forget about it. That doesn't happen with professional writers. They've got deadlines from editors and bills to pay. They don't have the luxury of feeling blocked.

That doesn't mean they always write well. Some days they don't. But they always, always write.

Here is what artist Chuck Close has to say on the subject:

> The advice I like to give young artists...is not to wait around for inspiration. Inspiration is for amateurs; the rest of us just show up and get to work. If you wait around for the clouds to part and a bolt of lightning to strike you in the brain, you are not going to make an awful lot of work. All the best ideas come out of the process; they come out of the work itself.

I think one thing that trips people up is that we are our own worst critics. It's hard to turn off that internal editor who tells you your stuff is junk. Endless second-guessing can be paralyzing.

So the key to getting over writer's block is to just write.

I'M NOT A GOOD COMMUNICATOR

There's a classic Chris Farley bit from *SNL*'s "Weekend Update."

He plays a rumpled character who bemoans his lack of interpersonal skills. As he catalogs his various deficiencies, he punctuates each one with great, sausage-fingered air quotes.

As I recall, it went something like this: "I'm not what they call 'camera friendly.' I'm not exactly 'telegenic.' I have 'bad teeth.' I don't 'bathe regularly.' I 'smell bad.' I 'frighten little children.'" And so on, in an ever-descending spiral of self-loathing.

Some executives and managers fear communicating because they compare themselves, ludicrously, to TV broadcasters and other communications professionals. But you don't have to be slick and media-savvy and quick on your feet to be an effective communicator.

More than anything else, you just need to be authentic. People respect institutional knowledge. Substantive experts, like engineers, love nothing more than hearing from someone they consider a peer—someone who can speak their language.

The most important thing is to just be yourself. To be sincere and real. That's something that can't be faked.

AN ACTOR AT WORK

Speed a Document to Approval

The approval process in some organizations can be maddening. If you're authoring a document, you've got to be like a football running back, protecting the ball and charging down the field, maneuvering around and, if necessary, running over tacklers to make your way to the end zone.

I have always believed there is little to fear from information. Opponents of communication—the tacklers in our analogy—are the lumbering beasts who have what might be called a bias for inaction. It's your job to overcome their objections through persuasion, if possible, or to thwart their efforts by marginalizing and going around them if necessary.

Otherwise, your document will get caught in a perpetual churn cycle, where people offer endless input instead of real value and mistake mindless activity for actual action.

Solutions include enlisting communication-friendly allies (the higher up in the organization the better), enforcing quick deadlines, demanding fast turnaround on approvals, and the old, "If we don't hear from you by [X] date/time, we'll assume it's okay to go forward."

Sometimes it's better to ask for forgiveness afterwards than permission beforehand.

Work Well with Lawyers

Whether you're seeking permission to answer a reporter's question, issue a press release, make an announcement or send out a document, you're often going to need the approval of lawyers. It's up to you to win their confidence and make them your allies instead of obstacles.

The key is to remember that attorneys have at least one natural, and very understandable, concern: liability. You need to allay that fear. You have to convince them that you're not going to make the problem worse.

I have worked with hundreds of lawyers. Many of them can actually be reasoned with. When I worked in the Attorney General's office, and the media or public were demanding answers on a sensitive case, we would sit down with the lawyers and come up with a response together. "Can we say this? What about this? How far can we go?"

In other words, start from a place of yes. There's

often more that can be said beyond "no comment," even if it's just the reason why you can't comment. A little context goes a long way in assuring people you're not just stonewalling.

Get Unblocked

Why are you reading this? I told you there is no such thing as writer's block.

Okay, here's the deal. You may be stuck, unable to write the thing you want or need to write, but that doesn't mean you can't write *something*. And that's the key to breaking out of a funk. It's like loosening up your muscles—once you get warmed up, your workout will be easier.

Here are a few tips for turning your brain cramp into a writer's cramp:

1 WRITE SOMETHING ELSE. An e-mail, a blog post, a grocery list. Anything to get a little momentum going.

2 FREE ASSOCIATE. Put pen to paper or fingers to keypad and write continuously for fifteen minutes without stopping. Seriously. Whatever comes to mind. What you had for breakfast, what you see in front of you. Just do it.

3 TRY SOME CREATIVE WRITING. Write about your childhood home, your first memory, a favorite teacher or best friend. Turn on the TV. Take a line of dialogue you hear and use it as the starting point for a story.

4 GO ONLINE. Find something that really fires you up—sports, politics, the weather—whatever floats your boat or gets

your goat. Read the comments and you'll see how regrettably few people online are impeded by writer's block. Join what passes for debate there and post a comment of your own. You might find that all you really need is to stir the passions a little.

5 CHANGE THE SCENERY. Go somewhere else to write.

6 GET MOVING. Get up out of your chair and take a walk or go for a run. Get energized.

7 READ. Great writing inspires me. See what it does for you. Pull out a favorite book, or go online and track down the screenplay to a favorite movie.

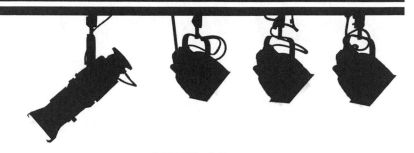

SCENE 15
ALWAYS BE REHEARSING

"All the real work is done in the rehearsal period."
—DONALD PLEASENCE

f you've spent any time at all watching the Oscars or Emmys, you've undoubtedly noticed how often the presenters screw up what would seem to be a pretty simple task.

They flub their lines, lose their place, read their co-presenter's parts, mispronounce names, fumble with envelopes, call people to the stage who aren't in attendance, and, when it's all over, exit the stage in the wrong direction, only to be dragged to the other side by a helpful lady in an evening gown.

And these are professional performers! "How could this be?" you may ask. There are a couple of explanations.*

First, performing live is a far cry from performing on film, where you have your lines memorized, multiple

---

* *One explanation, especially if it's the Golden Globes, where the drinks flow freely, is that they're probably drunk!*

chances to get it right, and far fewer people watching you and betting on how badly you'll screw things up.

Second, and more importantly, they either don't take the time to rehearse or they don't take the rehearsal process seriously. Perhaps they're divas who can't be bothered or maybe they assume since they're professionals they don't need it.

Rehearsal: It's for Everybody

Everybody needs to rehearse. Including you. Whether you're delivering a speech to three thousand people in a ballroom or doing a PowerPoint presentation for a few colleagues at a meeting, rehearsal is essential.

You need to practice your delivery, time things out, work through the transitions and, depending on the complexity of the event, get comfortable on the stage, work though any sound, music or lighting cues, and practice with the teleprompter.

The Kindness of Strangers

I've attended some pretty chaotic rehearsals. Not in my acting career—those are usually well organized, and everyone knows to pay attention to the director. With business people, it's different. Especially with high-level executives who may be distracted or aren't accustomed to taking instruction from, well, anyone—let alone strangers organizing an event.

But it's important to listen to the staff. They are trying to help you avoid making a fool of yourself.

Remember Dan Quayle? Labeled a political lightweight, he suffered a very rough introduction onto the public stage. At one point, he followed an instinct natural to many people under stress: he lashed out at those around him, blaming them for his problems.

Quayle told his handlers to back off, and they obliged, with wholly predictable results. At the next big event on the schedule, they watched from the sidelines as he, in the anonymously sourced words of an advisor, which I have paraphrased here, proceeded to step on a very delicate part of his own anatomy.

A chastened Quayle decided thereafter to be more open to counsel.

Politics is a particularly brutal business, but the lesson still applies: you want your staff on your side, working and rooting for you, not reveling in your downfall.

PREPARATION IS KEY

Beyond the mechanics of stagecraft, the most critical factor in grounding your "performance" and delivering your material with poise and confidence is to know your stuff. The better you know your material, the more comfortable you're going to be.

In theater, we do five or six weeks of rehearsal before opening a show, and though it never seems like enough time, it's a real luxury compared to business, where you might get, at most, a few days or maybe a week for a really big event.

Make the most of your formal rehearsal time, and supplement it by practicing at home if necessary.

DON'T SABOTAGE YOURSELF

I've seen so many executives squander their narrow window of rehearsal time by making endless revisions to their slides and text. At a big conference where there are lots of moving parts—light and sound cues, teleprompter, visuals, other speakers—the material really should be locked down and finalized twenty-four hours beforehand.

Every change that's made at the last minute increases exponentially the chance for error during the performance. I've spent a lot of time backstage at these events where people are frantically working to update slides and scripts just minutes before a presentation is to start.

These people are human, they get stressed out, they make mistakes. To say nothing of the very likely chance of a computer crashing when there's no time to spare.

So take it easy on them and make it easy on yourself. Stop futzing with the content and focus on your performance.

BEYOND PERFORMANCE: SIX EASY STEPS

Rehearsal is about more than your delivery. It's about planning ahead for desired outcomes. You should prepare carefully for every interaction that's important to you—networking events, client lunches, even one-on-one meetings.

That means determining your goal up front, getting your "story" down and anticipating any questions or objections that may arise.

This doesn't have to be an overly complicated process. And after a while, it'll even become second nature. Here are six simple steps to help you be more prepared for any performance, large or small:

1 DETERMINE YOUR GOAL. Be specific. Do you want to make a sale, gain a contact, get a piece of information, do a favor, convince people to change how they do things? If you're not pursuing an actionable goal, what's the point of being there?

2 FIGURE OUT WHAT YOU WANT FROM THEM. Whether you're meeting with one person or speaking to a hundred, determine what you need them to do for you to achieve your goal.

This is a big thing in acting. We are taught that every person, in every interaction, *wants* something. It sounds a little cynical, but it's true. It may be something concrete—*hire me, lend me money, love me, pick up your clothes, pay attention.* Or it could be more subconscious: we may want to impress or punish or comfort or cajole.

In a performance, if you're not "playing the want" nothing seems at stake and the audience loses interest. In business, if you don't give your audience something to do, they'll walk away thinking, "So what?"

3 PREPARE YOUR STORY. Think of three key points or messages that support your goal and that will resonate with your audience. It doesn't have to be three, but it shouldn't be more than four or five. People can only remember so much. Grouping your information into a small handful of categories helps them process it easier.

4 ANTICIPATE OBJECTIONS. Spend some time thinking over the hard questions they may ask and how you'll respond. When I was working for the attorney general, we would assemble vast briefing books for big events like meetings with newspaper editorial boards. It was a long and sometimes frustrating process.

During one of these prep sessions an issue came up. The AG said we should put together some background and analysis on the subject. It was late and I was tired and I sort of whined, "Come on, do you really think they're going to ask that?" And he replied, sarcastically and hilariously, "You're right. And if it does come up, I'll just say, 'I'm sorry, I don't have a good answer for that because my press secretary assured me you wouldn't ask about it.'"

So yes, play devil's advocate and think of the toughest questions they may ask.

5 VISUALIZE THE SITUATION. Not everybody finds this helpful, but I do. I like to imagine the setting I'll be in. A restaurant, an office, a conference room. Then I just "walk through" the expected sequence of events in my mind. For whatever reason, it helps me feel more comfortable and prepared.

6 PRACTICE. This gets back to the performance side of things, but it's the essential final step. Practice. Aloud, if possible. It may not make perfect every time, but it definitely increases your odds for success.

A CAVEAT

In the improv world, you're often warned not to get too much "inside your head." That means you're over-thinking things and not being open to the moment.

We used to play a terrifying group game called "freeze tag," where everyone stands along the back wall of the stage while a couple of people perform a short scene up front. When someone says, "Freeze," the performers literally stop in their tracks and replacements step up, adopt their poses and start a brand new scene.

The people who do best at this game come in with no pre-conceived ideas. They just step up, assume the position and say or do whatever comes into their head at the moment. The worst thing you can do in freeze tag is sit back and wait for the perfect opportunity to shoehorn into the show the brilliant bit you thought up on the back wall. In this situation, pre-planning almost never works.

So be careful not to over-prepare to the extent you're just rigidly pursuing an agenda. Opportunities and ideas arise from unexpected places and at unpredictable times, so it's important to be flexible and open to whatever may come along.

THE TWO PS

Rehearsal is equal parts *practice* and *planning*.

The practice should never stop. Even the performance itself is part of a process of continuous learning, adjustment and improvement. Which brings me to a quote from actor Martin Landau:

> **"** I always treat each take as a rehearsal for the next take. That way you can find stuff and keep adding and playing until they tell me to stop.

As for the planning part, there's a lot of truth in the old saying, "Most people don't plan to fail; they fail to plan."

AN ACTOR AT WORK

Prepare for a Speech

As I said, preparation is the most important thing you can do to assure a confident performance. But if you still have the jitters, try clearing your mind and focusing on the physical instead. Here are some warm-up exercises I find helpful:

■ *Stretching*. Hitting the stage with a high energy level is critical to grabbing and holding an audience's attention. The simple act of stretching, as you might do before a run or workout, is really helpful. Stretching loosens the body and gets the blood moving and the oxygen flowing. Working on the biggest muscles first, like the quads, gets the job done faster.

■ *Breathing*. Even though it's an autonomic function, most people don't breathe enough. Take note of your own breathing patterns sometime and you'll be surprised at how often you may be holding your breath during the course of the day. Especially when you're concentrating hard or under stress—which, of course, is exactly when you need oxygen the most. Before a presentation or speech, take several long, deep breaths. That will relax and ground you better than anything else.

■ *Vocal warm-ups.* I tend to talk quickly and sometimes stumble over or slur my words. Acting has taught me some great vocal exercises for limbering up my lips and tongue and making my diction more precise. My favorite is "Mike Ditka, Dick Butkus," because I drop my Ts too easily sometimes. Others include "Red leather, yellow leather," "Many mumbling mice are making midnight music in the moonlight— mighty nice," and any of the old childhood staples like "Fuzzy Wuzzy" and "Peter Piper."

Be a More Effective Networker

Whether you're at a formal networking event, a party, or just walking around town, you should always be prepared to describe who you are and what you do in a concise and compelling way.

You've probably heard of the elevator speech. It's a simple way to describe yourself in thirty seconds. If you don't have one prepared, here is a great template offered by a colleague, David Ryan of Gray Matters Group, who is an expert on networking and relationship building:

1 Who am I? (Introduce yourself.)

2 Who do I work for and what do I do?

3 What group of people do I service? (Be specific—do you have a niche?)

4 What unique value do I offer? What makes me different from the competition?

5 What benefits do my customers derive from my services?

Using this template, my elevator speech might be:

I'm Rob Biesenbach. I'm a communications strategist, an actor, and a writer. I help corporate clients and others communicate more effectively by taking techniques from the world of performance and applying them to business. It's a unique approach that helps clients stand out from the crowd through more creative tactics and programs.

As David advises, you should have a few different versions of your elevator speech on hand for different audiences—potential clients versus business partners, for instance. And it should never sound like an actual speech. It should be casual and conversational, with room to improvise, depending on the "audience."

Pitch Your Document

Really important documents deserve more than the typical review and approval process, where people just mark up changes and e-mail them around. Next time, try "pitching" it, like they do in Hollywood.

Here's how to do it:

1 Prepare a two-minute pitch based on your document that includes this information:

- Who's the audience?
- Where are they in terms of knowledge, perceptions, and mood?
- What's the goal of this communication?
- How does it address the audience's concerns?
- What are the top three points we're making?

2 Call a meeting to deliver the pitch. Start by providing any context or background necessary—earlier meetings or decisions that brought you to this point. Keep in mind that they haven't been immersed in the subject matter like you have, so they may need to be brought back up to speed. Present your pitch with confidence and enthusiasm. You are, after all, selling.

3 Ask if there are any questions and address any concerns people may have. Then proceed to hand out the document. For added emphasis, put your pitch in bullet points at the top of the first page. That can actually have a lot of influence—thankfully, some people really do believe everything they read.

Not only will this exercise help focus the people who are reviewing and approving the copy, it should help you sharpen the content yourself as you're developing it. There's nothing like an audience to keep you honest.

SCENE 16
FIND YOUR OWN PROCESS

f you look on the Internet, you will find no shortage of information about "the writer's process." There are thousands of articles and sites and blogs and books.

Much of it is geared to novelists or screenwriters or others from the creative world. As a result, a lot of the advice is impractical for business purposes.

After all, how useful is it for you to know that Hemingway wrote standing up? (Have you priced a standup desk lately? I bet your office manager will when you request one.)

Or that George Will believes that true writing can only occur with that direct connection of pen to paper? (Good luck finding someone to type up your chicken scratch these days. Even Don Draper is typing his own stuff now.)

Or that Sylvester Stallone only writes three hours a day? * ("Nope, it's not done, but *I* am!")

And just try putting your copy away and not looking at it for a few weeks or months or a year, as some recommend. ("Sorry, boss, you can't see the draft now, it's in my desk drawer, marinating.")

HIS WAY OR THE HIGHWAY

I've talked elsewhere about Robert McKee's *Story*. Screenwriters tend to view his tome with equal parts reverence and disdain.

Reverence because the guy's a legend—a longtime, successful industry veteran who clearly knows his stuff. Disdain because the process he advocates—adhering to a strictly prescribed structure and spending months outlining your story on scores of little notecards, among other things—has caused countless aspiring writers to give up in despair without ever putting a line of dialogue on paper.

McKee doesn't tell you his way is the only way. But he also reminds you at every turn that this is a tried-and-true process that has proven successful for Hollywood's most sought-after screenwriters. His not-so-hidden message: ignore my advice at your own peril.

If you're at all interested in the topic, check out the movie *Adaptation*. It beautifully depicts the writer's struggle and contains a hilarious send-up of McKee's methods. McKee actually makes an appearance as himself in the movie, and it's not entirely clear whether he's in on the joke.

The point is, listen to what others have to say about process, but figure out what works for you. I first got an inkling of my "process" in junior high.

WRITING LIKE A SEVENTH GRADER

On the first day of seventh grade English class, the teacher told

---

* *Yes, this is probably the first and last time Ernest Hemingway and Sylvester Stallone are mentioned so closely together, but Sly actually won an Oscar for his first Rocky screenplay.*

us we were going to write one essay every week. Most of the class groaned, but I thought, "What a great way to redeem myself from the daily humiliations of gym class!"

But even I griped when I heard about the process she had in store for us. We would develop our essay throughout the week, with each day devoted to a different phase. Monday was for brainstorming, Tuesday for outlining, Wednesday rough draft, Thursday second draft, and on Friday we polished and turned in the final draft.

I tried to work within the constraints of her system, but after a couple of weeks I found myself quickly settling on an idea on Day 1 then writing the whole essay then and there.

But since she demanded to see all five stages of the process, the rest of my week was spent forging the appropriate documents—boiling down the essay into a series of Roman numerals and letters and creating fake rough drafts with plausible-looking cross-outs and margin scribbles.

For the most part, I still write like this. If I create an outline it's usually only for the client's benefit—part of the approval process for going forward. And as I go along, the drafts don't usually change too radically, unless the client completely changes his or her mind about what they want.

Putting the Pieces Together

How do you figure out your own process? You can read books and take workshops, but ultimately it's like any other process, from weight loss to people management: you have to put together the bits and pieces of advice that work best for you.

An excellent lesson comes from the old job-hunting guide, *What Color Is Your Parachute?* To figure out what you want to do in your career, the book advises you to think about those times when you were happiest and doing your best work. Then seek out opportunities that offer those conditions.

It's the same with the writing process. Think about those times when you've done your best writing, where it's flowed almost effortlessly.

What time was it? Where were you? What were the conditions? Pay attention to those things and a process will begin to emerge.

ONE GUY'S PROCESS

To get you started, here are some of the things I've noticed that work for me:

> ■ *Just for openers.* The vast majority of my time and mental energy is spent coming up with the opening—the first paragraph or, for longer documents, the first section. That introduction is so important to everything that follows. It sets the tone and direction, previews the content and suggests a structure. When I'm happy with the opening, I feel like the rest is just hanging ornaments on a Christmas tree.
>
> ■ *One foot in front of the other.* I prefer to write sequentially. One paragraph at a time, one after the other, in order. Who doesn't? But we don't always have this luxury. At the PR firm, especially, it was rare to have all the information we needed exactly when we needed it. So I had to adapt and complete what I could, leaving big holes here and there to fill in later. Some people do that as a matter of course. If it works for you, that's perfectly okay.
>
> ■ *Concentration.* I know people who can't write unless they're in a crowded room or have music blaring in their ears. I require good-sized chunks of quiet, uninterrupted time when I write—time that is almost impossible to find in an office setting. So when I work in a busy office I come in before everyone else, or write from home in the morning, or leave the office and take my laptop somewhere else. At minimum, I close the door, forward my phone to voice mail, and silence my e-mail notifications.

■ *Top of the morning.* We all have a time of day when we're at our most energetic. That's probably also the time you'll do your best writing. I write best in the morning. My personal theory is it's because I'm just coming from that weird dream-state, where anything seems possible. I haven't yet had a chance to get beaten down by a day's worth of obstacles, rejections and frustrations. My inner editor—the skeptic, the naysayer—is not quite awake yet. Maybe yours knocks off early and you're a night owl.

■ *Or the evening.* On the other hand, don't get into a rut. I always thought I was no good at writing late in the day. I would do it when necessary, but it was always a difficult, painful struggle. With work and other demands, I've had to write most of this book in the afternoons and evenings. And it's gone really well. So that's been eye-opening for me. Be careful of old habits.

■ *Inspiration.* I get some of my best ideas away from the computer. I write paragraph after paragraph of copy in my head when I'm in the shower or on the bike or at the gym. (I wrote a good chunk of this chapter on a bike ride, actually.) When I get inspired like this I dictate the copy into my voice mail or my phone's voice memo app. Because when we lose an idea, it can be lost forever.

■ *Sleep on it.* When I get to the end of a long draft, especially when it's late in the day, I try to wait until morning before sending it to others. I'm usually too burned out to edit and proof it right then, and I find that a night's sleep brings a much-needed fresh perspective. So when I agree to deadlines, I usually make them in the morning instead of the afternoon.

GO YOUR OWN WAY

The only "right" way to write is the way that works for you. Morning, noon, or night. "Mad genius" style with cocktail-napkin scribblings or thoughtful and careful and orderly. Crowdsourced or hermit-like.

Find your own way. And if it works, don't let anyone tell you differently. Not your boss, not your seventh grade teacher, not even Sylvester Stallone.

AN ACTOR AT WORK

Hunt and Gather More Efficiently

Before the writing comes the research phase. How you conduct it depends a lot on your personality and work style.

I had a colleague who was my complete opposite. I'm analytical, and she's more intuitive. Nowhere was this more evident than at the starting point of a project. We would each sit down with a giant stack of research and materials, but we'd tackle it in completely different ways.

I'd go into my office and pore through it all—every page—highlighting stuff, taking notes, organizing, and prioritizing. After several hours of total immersion I'd have a pretty good idea of what it all meant and how we could structure the information into a program or product.

She, on the other hand, would rifle through the documents as if she knew exactly what she was looking for. And she would fairly quickly identify the one or two concepts or ideas that would form the foundation of what we would produce.

I admire her approach but I haven't been able to duplicate it. I don't want to miss something important by skimming information. For me, the truth emerges from the details. Similarly, my approach likely wouldn't work for her. All that additional data wouldn't tell her anything she didn't already know. Yet both approaches are equally valid.

You have to discover by trial and error what works for you.

Write Alone, Write Apart

For me, writing is a solitary exercise. After reviewing materials and interviewing a few people, I like to go off by myself and bang out the copy.

Other people are more collaborative. They bring a group together at the outset to brainstorm ideas, they check in repeatedly throughout the process, and seek feedback from a large circle of reviewers.

Maybe it's the difference between being an introvert and an extrovert.

Obviously there's a time and place for either approach. For me, written materials are the best source of data and people are best for providing texture—the context, framework and stories that help bring whatever you're writing to life.

But I've also seen perfectly good documents groupthinked and committed to death. And this desire to constantly expand the circle of input is often a thinly disguised exercise in butt covering.

As the writer, you are ultimately responsible.

ACT VI VI VI VI V

THE BIG PICTURE

"It's all one film to me. Just different chapters."
—Robert Altman, film director

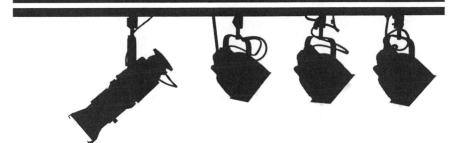

IN THE SPOTLIGHT

few years ago I took a short workshop on auditioning skills (yup, there's a class for everything). I arrived, as I often do, with barely a minute to spare. I briskly greeted the person who buzzed me in and rushed past her for the stairway, listening over my shoulder for directions to the classroom.

I took the stairs two at a time, got inside, scribbled through the requisite forms, grabbed a seat and caught my breath as I waited for things to start, grateful that at least several others trickled in after me.

The instructor began by reminding us that, as clearly stated in the course description, this class would be conducted like an actual audition. Which meant that all the normal auditioning rules apply, and the class actually started before we even got in the door. So "on time" means ten minutes early and the jeans I was wearing weren't appropriate.

Oops.

How we greeted the staff at the door was even part of the audition. Which we all should have known. Practically every director has a story (and maybe it's the same story passed around) about the actor who didn't get the job because he was rude to the person at the front desk. (At least I was courteous, if not exactly warm and indulging.)

It was a vivid reminder of the old adage that you're always auditioning. Always. At the sign-in desk (do you treat the receptionist like a human being worthy of respect?), in the waiting room (do you spend your time griping about the process?), even later on when gathering with friends (do you gossip about people in the business?).

Because you never know who's watching or listening.

HOT MIKE

The equivalent rule in the communications business is to assume that the microphone is always on. Incredibly, politician after politician (as well as CEOs and even professional newscasters) forget this on a regular basis. Happily, they provide wonderful YouTube fodder for the rest of us to enjoy.

Remember the network news anchor who went to the restroom accompanied by her live microphone, which dutifully broadcast on live TV her entire bathroom conversation, including her complaints about her "control freak" sister-in-law? You don't? Don't worry, it's on the Internet. Where it will live forever.

OH, AND ABOUT THAT INTERNET ...

The ever-increasing levels of transparency and connectedness that are a fact of life in this world present more and more opportunities to embarrass ourselves and put our careers in jeopardy.

A couple of years ago there was the story of the big-city PR exec who went to visit a client in Memphis. Shortly after arriving, he issued a semi-disparaging tweet about the town, which didn't go over so well with the client, who inevitably found out.

Things were eventually smoothed over, but not without a good deal of awkwardness and negative attention. It was an unnecessary distraction that could have been avoided with just an extra moment's consideration before hitting the enter key.

THE EARS HAVE IT

Another smart self-preservation move is to assume someone is always listening, whether you're in the office elevator, at Starbucks, or on the phone. Having spent time in government and politics, I've long been conditioned to this reality.

In the early days of car phones, there were cases I recall of ham radio operators randomly (and sometimes not so randomly) picking up the conversations of politicians and turning over the tapes to the media or competing political operatives. Headlines and even indictments ensued.

WATCH WHAT YOU DO

Just as actions speak louder than words, it's not just about what you say; it's also about what you do, particularly when it comes to your customers or clients. As representatives of our companies, we are always "on," even when we're away from the microphone. Or away from the workplace.

Always, always, always.

In the agency business there's the possibly-apocryphal-but-nonetheless-chilling story of the young account guy who was seen by his client patronizing a competitor's business. The agency was immediately fired. So, obviously, if you're working for Miller you should not be seen ordering a Bud Light in a bar. (And claiming you were doing "competitor research" usually won't cut it.)

I was acutely aware of this heightened scrutiny when I worked in the attorney general's office. Doing stupid things in public, hanging around with the wrong people, breaking the law—all bad ideas.

Bridging the acting and business worlds, there was the case of the GEICO voiceover actor who was fired after leaving a drunken voicemail message at the offices of a Tea Party group. A commenter online wondered why GEICO should care—they're owned by Berkshire Hathaway and Warren Buffet's a pretty liberal guy, he reasoned.

Nonsense. Warren Buffett's a businessman. As are the people running GEICO. It doesn't matter whether they personally agree or disagree with the viewpoint expressed. The point is, businesses don't like controversy.

They're paying very dearly to communicate their brand and the last thing they want is something that distracts from those efforts. Or that alienates any portion of their customer base.

It's the same reason why a major beverage company was disturbed to learn that one of the actors in its network TV commercials was also appearing in late-night cable spots for a certain adult personal lubricant.

How unfair, you may say. Isn't this America? Yes, it is still America, But in the words of Hymen Roth in *The Godfather: Part II*, "This is the business we've chosen."

The best advice is to follow an old PR axiom: for anything you say, write, or do, imagine how it would look on TV or in the news. Remember, it's always on. And so are you.

AN ACTOR AT WORK

Don't Blow the Interview Before You Get It

It's common practice now for potential employers to research job candidates online. What does your online presence say about you?

And they're not just looking at your LinkedIn profile. They're Googling you, checking out your Facebook page (including photos), reading your blog and tweets, watching your YouTube videos, wading through your message board posts.

Today's world presents you with two choices. First, you can try as much as possible to protect your privacy. Make maximum use of privacy controls, separate friends from business contacts, use nicknames for message boards and comments.

But some social media experts argue that these steps are pointless. Everything is moving toward greater openness and transparency, they say, so we all might as well get used to the reality of a life lived publicly.

Which brings us to your second option: change your behavior. Don't post anything you wouldn't want your employer to see. Don't say anything about people that you wouldn't say to their face. Don't do bad or embarrassing things.

That's a tall order, of course. It's possible that the growing futility of controlling our online image will lead to greater acceptance and tolerance. Who knows?

Whatever this brave new world may bring, approaching it with a healthy dose of paranoia isn't a bad strategy.

Watch What You Send

It's amazing the things people will say—or send—in e-mail, texts, and direct messages. It's important to understand that both in your personal and business life, nothing you send online should be considered private. It's just too easy for it to end up in the wrong hands. And you don't have to be famous to be a target.

For example, there's the story of the California man charged in an elaborate hacking scheme that resulted in the public dissemination of nude photos of nearly two hundred women. It seems he trolled around on strangers' Facebook pages, where he found their e-mail addresses listed in their profiles.

He then gleaned enough personal information about them (birthday, pet's name, mother's maiden name, etc.) to guess their e-mail passwords. From there he hacked into their e-mail accounts, searched through the "sent" folders and found messages with compromising photos these women sent to significant others and spouses.

Then he sent the photos to every contact in the victims' address books. Or posted them to their Facebook pages. Imagine the reactions of these peoples' bosses, customers, and grandmothers.

There are so many lessons here it's hard to know where to start. First, of course, would be to not send compromising photos of yourself to anyone. Even without creepy hackers, you never know who might someday turn from friend to enemy.

Second, tighten your Facebook page's privacy settings. Think twice about even including your e-mail address—if people want to contact you, they can always message you through Facebook. And third, don't pick such easily guessed passwords.

This is an extreme case, of course, but it doesn't take a malicious character to expose your personal information. Accidents happen. And nothing on the Internet is truly, safely, 100 percent private.

Exercise Discretion with Business E-mail

Every major modern scandal, from Enron to Madoff, unearths a treasure trove of compromising e-mails. Otherwise known as "evidence for the prosecution."

Just like with your personal accounts, business e-mail should never be considered private. Obviously, the same goes for memos, or anything else written down for that matter. Even voice mail is fair game.

The Wikileaks document dumps are just one more indication that total privacy in this world is never assured.

But you don't have to be the subject of an indictment or some public scandal to be compromised. More often than not, major embarrassments are the result of simple carelessness—misapplication of the "reply all" option, hitting "send" prematurely, or selecting the wrong e-mail address.

So Rule Number One is to never put anything in writing that you wouldn't want the subject of the message to see. That includes gossip about a co-worker, criticism of a customer, even reservations about a product.

Stuff like, "It's not my fault—the client's an idiot who doesn't know what he wants" and "We're under budget on this account, so find something to do—anything—and bill, bill, bill!" and "Yeah, the product's got serious problems, but let's hope they don't notice before we get a chance to fix it."

Save these kinds of thoughts for conversation. Or express them in a way that doesn't sound so awful. The customer is "demanding" or "tough to please." Staff members are encouraged to "maximize their productivity." And "we're working on improvements."

The world is full of both malice and ineptitude. Why expose yourself to unnecessary risk?

SCENE 18

COMMUNICATION DRIVES STRATEGY

t's often said (and just as often debated) that theater is a writer's medium and film is a director's medium.

A playwright's words are near-sacrosanct. You just don't mess with them. You don't cut them, you don't change them, you don't even turn them into contractions to make them easier to say.

In film, on the other hand, once a screenplay has been sold, the writer's influence pretty much comes to an end. The director exercises free rein, dropping scenes, changing dialogue, and even bringing in other writers. And that's all before the editor starts slicing and dicing the story.

ONE WRITER'S POWER

There are exceptions, of course. A screenwriter with a shelf full of Oscars wields considerably more influence. Which Shia LaBeouf found out while filming Oliver Stone's *Wall Street: Money Never Sleeps*. Here is how he described it to reporters at the movie's premiere:

> **"** Josh Brolin and I are shooting this bike scene. And at one point I say to Josh a line: 'You should look at yourself in the mirror first and see yourself. It might scare you.' I looked at the line for a couple of months and thought I'd go to Oliver and say, 'You look at the mirror and look at yourself. It's sort of repetitive. Why don't we just cut one of those? Why don't I say, Look at yourself. It might scare you.' This is Oliver verbatim. He looks at me and goes, 'I like mirror. I wrote Scarface. Go f**k yourself.'

And writers the world over stood up and cheered.

MORE THAN AN AFTERTHOUGHT

Unfortunately, most business communicators don't enjoy that kind of power. In many organizations, they are viewed as mere documenters of other peoples' ideas and words and dutiful recorders of their inevitable edits.

In the same way, the communications process is not often thought of or used as a strategic tool. It's an afterthought—simply a way to disseminate strategy and policy instead of an essential means for devising them.

But it should—and can—be different. A client once said that "communication drives strategy." Meaning that communications should be an integral part of the policy and strategic development process from start to finish.

And in her company it was. She was one of the CEO's closest advisors, and her team was in on the ground floor of just about every important operational initiative that happened.

WORDS TO ACTION

Our major breakthrough started in the usual way. The company had paid a ton of money to one of the big management consulting firms to help them develop their business strategy. After six months, many meetings, and millions of dollars, they were left with a big, fat six-inch-thick binder. *Here's your strategy! Good luck!*

That's when we were called in. Our job was to communicate the strategy. The problem was, even after all that work, the executives themselves couldn't really articulate it well.

So we became more than communicators. We were partners, working together over weeks and weeks, in an iterative process, to articulate the strategy. We slogged our way through the binder and churned out drafts and jotted bullet points on white boards.

And we talked. And talked and talked.

In six weeks we turned that big binder into a five-bullet-point strategy (with plenty of supporting information). The consultants were amazed at our handiwork. And that's how the strategy was truly born.

OUT OF YOUR HEAD

We've all met people who talk effusively about the great novel or screenplay or song they're working on. And when you ask them how the writing is going, they tell you that, while they haven't actually started writing it yet, rest assured, it's all "up here," in their head.

That's not a novel or a screenplay or a song. That's just an idea.

It's the same with strategy. If it's all in your head, or in some great big binder, but you can't reduce it to words—a couple of paragraphs or a few simple bullet points—then you don't really have a strategy at all.

Running these ideas through the communications process helps define, organize, and refine them.

Or, in the words of Karl Kraus, "Language is the mother of thought, not its handmaiden."

And who is Karl Kraus, you may ask? He was a writer, naturally.

AN ACTOR AT WORK

Get Buy-in from Colleagues

When you need to get people aligned behind a strategy or policy, put it in writing.

Few people are really abstract thinkers. They need to physically see it on paper before they can intellectually grasp it, let alone evaluate and agree to it. Putting concepts into black and white and circulating them for all to see can be a real eye-opener. After days or weeks of discussion, suddenly everyone becomes hyper-aware of exactly what it is they're committing to.

To me it's like a covenant. *This is what we've agreed to, this is how we're going forward. Speak now or forever hold your peace.*

Debate ensues, revisions are made, and finally the contract is sealed. Everyone is on the same page, as it were. Management is aligned. No excuses, no backing out.

Enforce a Deadline

If you need to get big projects moving in a large organization, schedule their rollout to coincide with major meetings and conferences. After all, there's nothing like a good public shaming to drive productivity.

When I worked at the National Association of Attorneys General, we had three big national meetings a year where all fifty state AGs and their assistants would get together. So for the staff, every major project, report, or publication would inevitably be scheduled for a high-visibility unveiling at the next national meeting.

This was done to ensure that these projects got the full personal attention of the AGs (and to not-so-subtly demonstrate our value and justify our existence as a staff). But an important side effect was that it drove us to frenetic, backbreaking heights of productivity in the weeks and months before each conference.

As *Saturday Night Live* creator and producer Lorne Michaels once famously said, "We don't go on [the air] because we're ready, we go on because it's 11:30."

Drive Accountability

If you want to get something done, get a leader to commit to it on the record and in public. Or at least in front of employees.

It's an excellent enforcement mechanism. Once the gauntlet is thrown down, there's no backing out. The executive won't want to lose face and the people around him won't want to disappoint.

It works the other way around, too. I worked with a CEO who would take advantage of employee events to extract public commitments from his managers. If a problem was pointed out, he'd look for answers and get his people on the record with what they were going to do about it.

SCENE 19

CREATING CATHEDRAL BUILDERS

The first time I was on the set of a major feature film (I was just an extra), I was astounded by the huge number of people working on it.

First assistant director, second assistant director, camera people, lighting people, sound people, set dressers, hair, makeup, wardrobe, catering. But what amazed me even more than the sheer number of crew was that every person there seemed intensely focused and committed, no matter what their role.

There was a guy whose entire responsibility involved carrying around a large supply of different colored gaffer tape and applying it where needed. And another whose job was to corral us extras and shut us up when we were restless and noisy.

And when it came time for our scene, even though we were just background players, the assistant director took the time to tell us what the scene was about and how it fit in the context of the film.

It seemed like everyone had that perspective. No matter how incidental their responsibilities, they clearly felt they had a critical role in making that movie, and they did their jobs diligently and professionally.

I've been on plenty of dysfunctional sets, but this one was a veritable case study in employee engagement, an area of communications that can have a truly transformational impact on organizations and people.

TEN WAYS TO TRANSFORM THE ORGANIZATION THROUGH COMMUNICATION

1 BE FIRST

Whether you're managing a media crisis or implementing major changes in the workplace, you want to be the first to tell your story. Your employees, certainly, want to hear news from you before seeing it online or on TV.

Don't pretend this outside world doesn't exist or has no influence. I recall a memo from the management of a public company that was going through a major earnings restatement crisis. It advised employees to disregard everything they were hearing from outsiders, saying, in a major case of wishful thinking, "If you don't hear it from us, it's not true."

A company that values its employees keeps them informed. And a company that values its reputation gets out ahead of the story.

I always compare the first version of a story to a stake in the ground. Everything that's said after that is measured against it. Absent some kind of bombshell revelation, we'll never succeed in pulling that stake up and moving it into our own favorable territory. More often than not, if we didn't plant that stake ourselves, the most we can do is try and bend it back in our direction.

2 PAINT THE PICTURE

What does the competitive landscape look like? Where do we fit in? What are the challenges we face? What are the threats and opportunities?

Without context, people are operating in a vacuum. Don't assume they're interested only in those things that immediately affect the work they do.

3 PROVIDE DIRECTION

Where are we going? What is the vision or goal? What is the strategy for getting there?

Successful communication identifies that point on the distant horizon that we're aiming for. So even during the inevitable zigs and zags of the daily journey, people will understand and see that they're on course.

4 DEFINE THE STAKES

What happens if we succeed? What are the consequences of failure? What, specifically, is in it for everyone?

Make it personal. A fluctuation in market value is abstract (unless people have an ownership stake). Future financial bonuses or potential job losses are tangible.

Make it big. People need a rallying cry. Though it's a little dramatic, it's been said that people will work for a company, but they'll die for a cause.

5 GIVE THEM A ROLE

Everyone wants to feel that they're part of something bigger than themselves. Everyone can contribute more than they're asked.

Draw a clear connection between each person's job and how it advances the larger strategy.

6 PROVIDE INCENTIVES

There's an old HR saying: show me how someone behaves and I'll show you how they're paid. If management is telling people they need to work in teams across departments but doesn't give them any financial incentive to do so, then it's just talk. Money is not a primary motivator for everyone, but few people are going to work against their own financial interests.

Incentives have to be aligned with desired behaviors. Otherwise, your efforts are doomed.

7 LISTEN

Provide a wide variety of opportunities for people to have a voice. Town halls, committees, surveys, Intranet, social media, open door policies.

When issues are raised, document them. Help see to it that the issues are addressed and that employees are kept informed of any progress. It's amazing how fixing one small problem can affect outlook and motivation.

And even if they don't get the answers they want, people appreciate being heard.

8 GIVE FEEDBACK

Everyone wants to know how they're doing. Tell them.

And do it in a tactful way. That doesn't mean papering over an ugly truth, it just means treating people with respect, which not only is the right thing to do, it's more effective. People aren't likely to listen when they feel they're being insulted.

So package the feedback within something more positive and encouraging, such as, "I appreciate how quickly you turn assignments around, but the last couple of times they've come back with a few errors. I just want you to know that speed isn't necessarily as important as quality."

Don't speculate on behaviors; talk about results. Wrong: "This report was really sloppy—didn't you bother to proofread it?" Right: "I've noticed a number of errors in your work lately, which is really unusual for you. What's happening, and how can I help?"

It's not a matter of being touchy-feely—it's about treating people right.

9 SHOW YOU CARE

Acknowledge peoples' frustrations, fears and anxieties. If those feelings are shared, show it. Express concern. Promise to do all you can. A simple gesture of sincere compassion and genuine empathy can cover a multitude of sins.

10 WALK THE TALK

Actions speak louder than words. Leaders need to model the behaviors they seek in others. More than what we say, people watch what we do.

DON'T SETTLE FOR ROCK BREAKERS

Back at the PR firm, we used to tell this story when talking about the employee communications practice:

> A man walks past a construction site and sees three people doing the same job. He asks each of them what they're doing.
> "I'm breaking rocks," said the first.
> "I'm earning a living," said the second.
> The third one replied, "I'm helping build a cathedral."

That story has become a bit of a chestnut (believe me, back in the day it was groundbreaking stuff), but more than anything else—more than diagrams and flow charts and bullet points—it captures the power of internal communications to transform organizations.

Cathedral builders are always going to be more engaged, more effective, more valuable than rock breakers.

AN ACTOR AT WORK

Rally a Team

If you want to get buy-in for your ideas, you need to demonstrate a decent level of excitement yourself. And if you want your people to follow you over that hill, you need to show them what's at stake.

Invest your pitch with emotion. Appeal to people's pride. Explain the big picture and their role in it. Ask for their help. Give them something to do.

Most of all, tell them what they're fighting for.

Develop Employees

Some managers only think about employee development once a year when annual review time rolls around. But doing it properly requires an ongoing commitment, day in and day out.

The performance review is the bare minimum. It provides a blueprint. The strengths, weaknesses and goals identified there should guide everything from the assignment of new projects to the way teams are assembled.

But true employee development requires constant communication—checking in both on a periodic basis and whenever issues arise that provide an opportunity for feedback.

Get into the Trenches

Front-line employees can be a tough audience to please, but it's important to try.

The situation brings to mind the old joke Woody Allen tells in *Annie Hall*: two elderly women are dining out. One of them says, "Boy, the food in this place is really terrible," and the other replies, "Yeah, I know, and such small portions."

The attitude of front-line employees toward management is a lot like that. They don't like you, they don't trust you, they don't believe you care...and they don't see nearly enough of you.

There are lots of issues going on here. They feel far removed from the decisions that affect their lives, they feel like nobody listens to them.

What it mostly comes down to, though, is dignity and respect. (Which is why, incidentally, those two messages are front and center in any effort by labor unions to organize a workplace.)

Management can begin to address these issues by, first of all, getting out on the floor and talking face-to-face with employees on their turf. And it shouldn't be some phony "grip and grin" session. I worked with a CEO who went around asking people, "Tell me one thing we're doing right, and one thing we can do better." It was a simple way to make these interactions substantive and constructive.

Town hall meetings are another important tactic. Prepared remarks should be short and message-focused, illuminating the big picture and employees' role in it. Most of the time should be devoted to answering questions and engaging the audience in freewheeling conversation.

Giving people multiple channels—live and

electronic—to air their concerns, make suggestions, and interact with others is also critical. And, of course, actually addressing those concerns is vital.

Most of all, these efforts need to be sustained over time. People are wary of "flavor of the month" initiatives that get dropped as quickly as they start. Persistence is the only way to make a difference over the long run.

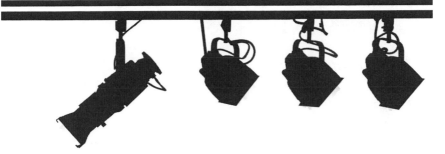

ENCORE

STAND UP, STAND OUT

 n an unforgettable *Simpsons* episode, Bart puts his red cap into a load of laundry, causing all of Homer's white shirts to come out pink. Mortified, but having no choice, Homer heads to work, where Mr. Burns and Smithers are monitoring security camera footage of employees entering the plant:

MR. BURNS: Why is that man in pink?

SMITHERS: That's Homer Simpson, sir. He's one of your boobs from Sector 7-G.

MR. BURNS: Simpson, eh? Well, judging by his outlandish attire, he's some sort of free-thinking anarchist.

> SMITHERS: I'll call security, sir.
>
> MR. BURNS: Excellent.

Poor Homer was given a psychological evaluation and promptly dispatched to a mental institution. He paid the ultimate price for standing out in corporate America. As the saying goes, "The nail that sticks up gets hammered down."

The fear of looking or being different is at the heart of the bland, ordinary communications that plague business today. And it's understandable. All our lives we're encouraged to conform. Who wants to risk getting hammered down? So we let fear and insecurity overrule our instincts.

FORGET YOUR FEAR

Actors are notoriously insecure creatures, and one guy who's seen more than his fair share of it is Mick Napier. As a director and instructor at Second City and his own Annoyance Theater, he has trained thousands of young comic actors, including Tina Fey, Rachel Dratch, and many others.

In a blog post titled "The Perfect Actor," he offers up some tough-love advice, including this pearl:

> [Forget] your fear.* We want to see your power, not your fear. Nobody has time for your fear...If I, as director, must constantly spoon-feed and suggest and coddle the actor in regard to their ideas, lines, and characters, then there's a 90% chance that the person is coming from a huge space

---

* *Mick actually used an earthier word than "forget," but you get the point.*

```
of insecurity. When I teach, I
expect insecurity; when I direct, I
expect the opposite.
```

We have evolved an incredible capacity for over-intellectualizing every little thing. Seeking to mitigate all risk in our lives and careers, we analyze, we weigh options, and we second-guess, sowing the seeds of doubt in ourselves and in others.

But some people don't have this problem. Think of the *American Idol* contestant who couldn't find the right key if he was lip-synching it. Do you think he's afraid of what others think?

Or the writer of the next Great American Novel toiling away for decades on her 300,000-word manuscript. Does she ever suffer from writer's block?

How about the guy who's more Kevin James than James Franco strutting across the gym locker room stark naked? You think he frets over society's conventional standards of beauty?

Hell, no, they don't!

What's their secret? Delusion.

Use Your Delusion

It's a major irony of this world that so many bright, creative people are plagued by near crippling self-doubt, while those who could benefit from a healthy dose of reality breeze right through, oblivious to their own limitations.

But instead of ridiculing them, maybe we could all use a little more delusion in our lives.

Think about that the next time you worry about adding a joke to your e-mail or delivering a speech on the fly. What is the risk, really? How many of us work under life-or-death conditions? Let go of the fears that limit you. Be bold. Stand out.

Another inspirational figure from the world of improv is Martin de Maat, who was a much beloved teacher and administrator at the Second City Training Center. He died in 2001, about a year before

I started taking classes there, but his presence in the building and among those who knew him is indelible.

By all accounts, he was a one-of-a-kind figure who put everything into his work, and he encouraged his students to do likewise. One of his favorite sayings was, "The Hokey Pokey. Think about it. At the end of the song, what do we learn? What is it all about?" (Dramatic pause, delighted grin.) *You put your whole self in!"*

Attack your communications and your work with passion and conviction. Hold nothing back.

Tell a story. Paint a picture. Put your heart into it. Connect. *Perform.*

Letting go of your fear is ultimately about believing in yourself.

Every organization could benefit from having a Martin de Maat around. His capacity to inspire and embrace, figuratively and literally (he was a generous hugger), was legendary. Though he nurtured numerous talents who went on to fame, including Chris Farley, Sean Hayes, and David Mamet, he saw something unique and valuable in every individual.

That philosophy is captured in something he would often say, and which today is inscribed on a plaque at the training center. It makes an excellent closing to this book:

"You are pure potential."

CURTAIN CALL
ACKNOWLEDGEMENTS

"It is never too late to be what you might have been."
—GEORGE ELIOT

I am grateful to the Canadian National Railway, the Woods Hole Oceanographic Institute, and the Pro Bowlers Association, who had nothing to do with the writing of this book, but probably don't get all the acknowledgment they deserve.

These people also had no involvement with the book but provided a lifetime of laughter and inspiration: Lou Costello, Lucille Ball, Jackie Gleason, Peter Sellers, Mary Tyler Moore, Steve Martin, Michael O'Donoghue, David Letterman, Chris Elliott, Matt Groening, Jerry Seinfeld, Sarah Silverman, Steve Carell, Stephen Colbert, and Tina Fey.

Closer to home, my first real foray into performance came with classes at Second City Training Center. I'm grateful to the instructors and directors who taught me, especially the late, wonderful Mary Scruggs, who successfully walked the narrow tightrope of helping us be our best while taking care not to crush our souls.

Several friends and colleagues took a look at early drafts of the book and provided helpful feedback and, most of all, affirmation that I was onto something worth pursuing. Thank you to Dawn Doty,

Janine MacLachlan, Susanne Schnell, and Elena Zahorik.

My publishers and editors at Brigantine Media were important partners in shaping the content. Thanks especially to Janis Raye and Neil Raphel. This book wouldn't be half as good without their input and guidance.

The kids at my local Argo Tea, where I wrote much of the content, kept me infused with enough Tea Earl Grey Hot (in the famous phrasing of Captain Jean-Luc Picard) to keep me going in strong, yet Zen-like, fashion. I also received critical support from Michelle Byerley, Mike Tutaj, and the nice people at the Prop and Factory theaters.

Finally, one thing harder than writing a book is putting up with someone who's writing a book, so my everlasting gratitude goes to Karen Nelson for her encouragement and oft-tested patience.

About the Author

Rob Biesenbach is a communications strategist, an actor, and a writer. During his twenty-plus year career in communications and PR, he has counseled clients from Fortune 500 companies to startups.

He has managed a successful solo practice for more than a decade. Prior to that, he served as a vice president at Ogilvy PR Worldwide, press secretary to the Ohio Attorney General, and communications director for the National Association of Attorneys General.

Rob started his performance career in 2002, studying acting, improvisation, and writing at Second City Training Center and elsewhere. He has acted in more than 150 theatrical and commercial productions. He also wrote a collection of one-act plays, *The One-Eyed Cat & Other Tales of Need*, and a sketch revue, *There's No "I" in Improv*, which were staged at Donny's Skybox Theater at Second City.

Rob lives in Chicago with his allergies.

www.RobBiesenbach.com

Index